ESSAYS IN THE HISTORY
OF THE AMERICAN NEGRO

Essays in the History of the American Negro

Herbert Aptheker

NEW YORK

INTERNATIONAL PUBLISHERS

E
185
.A6
1964

ISBN 0-7178-0061-**X**

CONTENTS

PREFACE

The chapters in this volume originally appeared as four pamphlets published each year from 1938 to 1941. The first edition of the four issued in one volume appeared in 1945, and was reprinted in the following year; naturally, it is most gratifying to the author that the publisher finds continuing demand justifies a new edition.

In the early reprint and in this edition no changes have been made.

Tremendous progress has been achieved in the past generation in the Negro liberation movement; everything points to the conclusion that progress in the generation ahead of us will be at least as momentous. Part of the effort to cleanse the United States of racism is to cleanse its educational system of that blight. Certainly, an anti-racist educational system cannot have racist history books; integrated schools require integrated texts.

A basic part of the racist mythology is the denial that the African-derived peoples have had as significant a history as any other people and specifically the denial that the American Negro people have had a stirring history of their own and have also played central roles in the entire past of the United States. Accordingly, a basic part of the effort to smash that mythology must be the affirmation and the demonstration of the truth concerning Negro history. The present book is part of that effort; to the degree that it made any contribution towards the goal of equality in the past generation and may in the future, the author's efforts are sufficiently rewarded.

It may be helpful to indicate briefly some of the work in the history of the Negro people in the United States through the Civil War that has appeared since 1942.

Outstanding has been the writing of John Hope Franklin and of Benjamin Quarles, particularly, in the former case, the text, *From Slavery to Freedom* (New York, 1947), and *The Militant South* (Cambridge, Mass., 1956), and in the latter case, *The Negro in the Civil War* (Boston, 1953), *The Negro in the American Revolution* (Chapel Hill, 1961), and *Lincoln and the Negro* (New York, 1962). An important pioneering effort to place the Negro people within the whole context of U.S. history is William Z. Foster's *The Negro People in American History* (New York, 1954); the first three hundred pages deal with the period to 1865. Excellent is Kenneth M. Stampp's *The Peculiar Institution: Slavery in the Ante-Bellum South* (New York, 1956). Two important works on the antislavery movement—both of which do not neglect the role of the Negro therein—are: Louis Filler, *The Crusade Against Slavery* (New York, 1960) and D. L. Dumond's massive *Anti-Slavery: The Crusade for Freedom in America* (Ann Arbor, 1961). Two splendid anthologies on the same subject have come from Louis Ruchames: *A John Brown Reader* (New York, 1960), and *The Abolitionists* (New York, 1963). A ground-clearing work on the Negro in the pre-Civil War North was done by Leon F. Litwack, *North of Slavery* (Chicago, 1961).

In the period since 1942 the present writer published several works which dealt in whole or in part with the pre-Reconstruction history of the American Negro people. These include: *American Negro Slave Revolts* (first published in 1943; new edition, New York, 1963); *To Be Free: Studies in American Negro History* (New York, 1948); *A Documentary History of the Negro People in the U.S.* (Vol. I, New York, 1951, new edition, 1962); *Toward Negro Freedom* (New York, 1956); *And Why Not Every Man?: The Story of the Fight Against Negro Slavery in the U.S.* (Berlin, 1961).

HERBERT APTHEKER

March, 1964

viii

NEGRO SLAVE REVOLTS IN THE
UNITED STATES, 1526-1860

I. INTRODUCTION

The wholly erroneous conception of life in the old South which is still dominant in our movies and novels and textbooks was invented by the slaveholders themselves. They and their spiritual—and even lineal—descendants have written the history of American Negro slavery. These Bourbons have been motivated by a desire to apologize for and, more than that, to justify a barbarous social system. To do this, they have been forced to commit every sin of omission, falsification and distortion. That they have done their job well is attested by the fact that the monstrous myth created by them is believed by most people today.

The apologists and mythologists who are responsible for this distorted picture of the slave system acknowledge as their pioneer and leader the late Professor Ulrich B. Phillips, of Georgia. His attitude clearly presents the approach of the entire school. In one of his early articles (1905), Phillips referred to himself as a person who had "inherited Southern traditions." That by this he meant Bourbon traditions is indicated by his dedication of an early book (1908) "to the dominant class of the South." Since he openly affirms such an allegiance, it is easy to imagine what he says of the old South. To Phillips, under the slave system "severity was clearly the exception, and kindliness the rule." Indeed, at one point he places quotation marks around the word slavery, indicating that that harsh word is hardly the proper one with which to label the system he describes.

And the opinions of this "authority" on the people who

were enslaved are remarkable to behold. His works are filled with adjectives like stupid, negligent, dilatory, inconstant, obedient—used to describe the Negro. To Phillips the Negro people are cursed by "inherited inaptitude" and are "by racial quality submissive." Thus American slavery emerges as a delightful social system admirably contrived for the efficient and undisturbed subordination of an inferior people.

WHAT WAS AMERICAN SLAVERY?

But the fact of the matter is that American slavery was a horrid form of tyrannical rule which often found it necessary to suppress the desperate expressions of discontent on the part of its outraged victims. The fundamental point to bear in mind is that for ninety per cent of the years of its existence and throughout some ninety per cent of the area it blighted, American slavery was, as Karl Marx stated, "a commercial system of exploitation." That is, American slavery, on the whole, was a staple producing system dependent upon a world market. There was, therefore, no limit to the exploiting drive of the slaveowners. And this system was quite as subject to business cycles, or periods of so-called prosperity, depression and panic, as any other system of private gain dependent upon a world market.

The peculiar feature of this staple-producing agricultural system was the fact that the laborers were owned by, were chattels of, the bosses or slaveholders. And the slaveholders, like employers the world over, were in business—that is, ran cotton or sugar or tobacco plantations—for the gain they could drive out of their workers, whom they literally owned.

So that instead of the delightful picture of a patriarchal institution in which, as a Phillipsian professor recently put it, the slave "was assured of an income proportioned

4

to his necessities and not to his productiveness," one has a large-scale commercial system of exploitation in which the laborers were rationed out, in normal times, a bare minimum of their animal needs. Objection or resistance of any kind made the worker liable to any punishment his boss should decide was proper—sale, branding, lashing, or some other more excruciating form of torture.

Moreover, productiveness was a most important determinant of the amount of the rations. The plantation slaves were divided according to their productivity into full hands, three-quarter hands, half hands and quarter hands. The less productive workers, the children, the aged, many of the women, the less skilled or less strong received less to eat (often fifty or sixty per cent less) than did the more productive workers, or the "prime" field hands, as they were called.

When the depression and panic came to this staple-producing slaveholding system the workers—the slaves—suffered. James Madison explained, in 1819, what conditions affected slaves, and the first item he listed was "the ordinary price of food, on which the quality and quantity allowed them will more or less depend." Robert Hayne, a senator from South Carolina, while lamenting a depression in his native state, in January, 1832, declared that because of it the slaves were "working harder, and faring worse." A Charleston slaveholder, writing in 1811 in the midst of the economic hardships of the moment, stated, "The wretched situation of a large proportion of our slaves is sufficient to harrow up the feelings of the most flinty heart." John Randolph, a Virginia congressman, during the depression of 1814 and early 1815, felt that the slave "will suffer dreadfully" and noted his "tattered blanket and short allowance." At a time when Andrew Jackson was short of funds and depression prevailed, in 1841, he received word from his Mississippi plantation

5

that the slaves "were shivering and starving—provisions out and no shoes."

Other factors tended to worsen the slaves' condition. Soil exhaustion, for example, made the slaveholders drive their workers at a more rapid pace. Improvements expanding the market for plantation products, such as new industrial machines or better transportation facilities, had a like effect. A slave explained this, in the late 1850's, in blaming railroads for increased demand upon his labor, by remarking, "you see it is so much easier to carry off the produce and sell it now; 'cause they take it away so easy; and so the slaves are druv more and more to raise it."

LIVING CONDITIONS

These factors lowered the slave's general standard of living. But what was that standard? Hours of work were from sun-up to sun-down. Food consisted of corn and occasional meat or fish or molasses, with supplements from gardens, which some slaves were permitted to keep and which they might work in their "spare" time, as on Sundays. Another important supplementary source of nourishment came from what the slaves "took" from their masters. The masters called this stealing, but slaves felt themselves guilty of stealing only if they took the belongings of fellow slaves. Appropriating bread or milk or meat or clothing from the master was "taking," not stealing, for the slaves declared "as we work and raise all, we ought to consume all." Frequent application of this theory into practice was a great annoyance to the slaveholders, who decided that "stealing" was an inherent trait of the Negro. Surely the taking could not result from the slaves' need for more bread and meat and clothes!

Slaveholders, themselves, are the authorities for determining what they spent on their chattels' upkeep. One

6

cotton planter of fifteen years' experience, writing in the leading Southern periodical, that published by J. B. DeBow, declared that the masters' expense was often underestimated. He then proceeded to give what he thought was a proper estimate. The cost of feeding one hundred slaves for one year he said was seven hundred and fifty dollars—seven dollars and fifty cents *a year* for each slave's food—and this included the expenses of the "hospital and the overseer's table." The remaining items, clothing, shoes, bedding, sacks for gathering cotton, and other articles not enumerated also cost seven dollars and fifty cents per slave per year!

James Madison declared, in 1823, that the annual cost of a slave child in Virginia was from eight to ten dollars, and that the youngster became "gainful to his owner" at about nine or ten years of age. Forty-eight planters of Louisiana informed the United States Secretary of the Treasury in 1845 that the yearly expense of supporting the life of a prime field hand was about thirty dollars, and of others—children, aged, some women—fifteen dollars.

A good idea of the habitations of the field hands may be obtained from an article by a Mississippi planter, again in DeBow's publication. The gentleman's purpose in writing the article was to appeal for better slave housing —such as he provided. He owned one hundred and fifty slaves and provided them with twenty-four cabins, each sixteen by eighteen feet. That is, about six slaves "lived" in a hut sixteen by eighteen feet, and this condition was proudly held up for emulation!

THE QUESTION OF CRUELTY

Time and again modern readers are assured, as by Phillips, that cruelty was exceedingly rare under American slavery. The essential argument used is that it is absurd to believe that men would abuse their own slaves —their own property. Normal people, the apologists say, do not maltreat their cows or pianos; then why be cruel to a slave representing a value of several hundred dollars? Thus a biography, published in 1938 by Harvard University (S. Mitchell, *Horatio Seymour*, p. 103), declares that "owners were hardly likely to be cruel or careless with expensive pieces of their own property," just as most folks do not abuse their horses or automobiles.

It may first be remarked that society does find it necessary to maintain institutions for the prevention of cruelty to animals and to children, indicating the not infrequent existence of perverse, insane or malicious people. Slave society was certainly conducive to the production of such persons.

But, entirely apart from this first consideration, cruelty was an integral part of the slave system. The argument of interest would apply were the slaves horses or pianos or automobiles. But they were men and women and children. History certainly teaches us, if it teaches anything at all, that human beings have the glorious urge to be something better than they are at any moment, or to do something new, or to provide their offspring with greater advantages and a happier world than they themselves possess. People who are degraded and despised and sold and bought and arbitrarily separated from all that is familiar and dear will be unhappy. They will be discontented and will *think, at least, of bettering their conditions.* This last idea, if persisted in, was death to the slave institution, and it was precisely because the slaves were property, precisely because they were valuable and profitable, *but rational,* instruments of production, that cruelty was necessary.

Slavery was systematized cruelty. The slaves were machines to be driven as much as possible for the produc-

8

tion of profit, and machines of an intelligent nature which had to be terrified and chained and beaten in order for their owners to maintain possession. Specific examples of physical cruelty (taken from unimpeachable sources) are innumerable. At least a few of these, which indicate a general condition, deserve mention.

There was the case of Mr. Symon Overzee of Maryland and his slave, Tony. Tony staged a sit-down strike all his own--surely one of the first in America—way back in 1656. What happened was this: Tony ran away and was retaken with the aid of bloodhounds. He then waited only until his wounds healed and again fled. He was again captured. Flight being now impossible, Tony sat down and refused to rise. He would not work as a slave. Mr. Overzee bound him in an upright position by his wrists and proceeded to beat him. Tony still refused to serve as a slave. Mr. Overzee then poured hot lard over him, and Tony died. This procedure was rather irregular, and Mr. Overzee was brought before a court. He explained the facts and was acquitted by the court because Tony was "incorrigible."

The Grand Jury of Charleston, S. C., in 1816, presented "as a most serious evil the many instances of Negro homicide, which have been committed within the city for many years," and went on to refer to "the barbarous treatment of slaves" who were used "worse than beasts of burden."

A Mr. John Cooke was actually convicted in 1815 in North Carolina of the wanton murder of a slave under the most monstrous conditions. The Governor pardoned him. Said a native:

Some thought, as this was the first instance in which a white man had ever been convicted for killing a negro, it would be impolitic to hang him so unexpectedly. And others believing it would be wrong in all respects, to hang a white man for killing a negro. But whatever might have been the motives of his Excellency, we hear no dissatisfaction expressed by any at this act of clemency; yet we think it may be well to caution the unwary against the repetition of the too common practice of whipping negroes to death as...executive interposition may not be expected in all cases.

The British Consul in Charleston, S. C., wrote in a private letter of January, 1854:

The frightful atrocities of slave holding must be seen to be described.... My next door neighbor, a lawyer of the first distinction, and a member of the *Southern Aristocracy*, told me himself that he flogged all his own negroes, men and women, when they misbehaved.... It is literally no more to kill a slave than to shoot a dog.

As a final piece of evidence is offered the statement of a Major in the United States Army, Amos Stoddard, who lived in Louisiana from 1804 to 1809. In 1811 he wrote of that region:

cruel and even unusual punishments are daily inflicted on these wretched creatures, enfeebled, oppressed with hunger, labor and the lash. The scenes of misery and distress constantly witnessed along the coast of the Delta, the wounds and lacerations occasioned by demoralized masters and overseers, most of whom exhibit a strange compound of ignorance and depravity, torture the feelings of the passing stranger, and wring blood from his heart. Good God! why sleeps thy vengeance!

WHY THE REVOLTS?

Vengeance did not sleep. Bourbon historians, who have made slavery idyllic and the slaves an inferior people, have little place in their works for accounts of this vengeance—this heroic anti-slavery struggle of the Negroes. Thus, for example, Phillips in his latest work, published after his death, declared that "slave revolts and plots were very seldom in the United States"; and two other eminent historians recently said the same thing—John D. Hicks: "Attempts at insurrection were extremely rare"; James G. Randall: "Surprisingly few instances of slave insurrections."

The history of American slavery is marked by at least two hundred and fifty *reported* Negro conspiracies and revolts. This certainly demonstrates that organized efforts at freedom were neither "seldom" nor "rare," but were rather a regular and ever-recurring phenomenon in the life of the old South.

Considerable explanation of this rebellious activity has already been given. We have seen that cruelty—that is, actual physical maltreatment—was an essential part of slavery. We have seen that the system, in so-called normal times, provided a bare animal sustenance to its victims. And we have observed the fact that economic disaster seriously depressed the already miserably low standards of the Negroes.

Economic depression had other results of a disturbing nature. It would naturally sharpen the tempers of the slaveowners or of their overseers, whose incomes depended upon the value of the crop they could force the slaves to produce. Bankruptcy and liquidation are, moreover, concomitants of depression and, when property was human beings, its liquidation carried many stories of woe. For it entailed an increase in the leasing or sale of thousands of slaves, which meant the forced separation of brother from sister, child from mother, husband from wife. Surely it is more than a coincidence that the years of severe economic depression coincide with the periods of greatest rebellious activity.

Another factor of considerable importance in arousing concerted slave unrest was the occurrence of an exciting or unusual event. Thus, the landing of a new provincial governor from England in one of the colonies here might lead to a belief on the part of the slaves that they were to be freed, and thereby cause the masters trouble, as occurred in Virginia during 1730. Again, the prevalence of revolutionary philosophy and activity, as from 1770 to 1783, or the rapid spread and growth of an equalitarian religion, as Methodism from 1785 to 1805, or a war against a foreign power, as against Great Britain from 1812 to 1815, or stirring debates in Congress over the question of slavery, as in 1820, or particularly exciting Presidential campaigns as those of 1840 and 1856,—all clearly aroused subversive activity on the part of the slaves. The actual outbreak of a slave revolt seems also to have had a contagious effect, so that, for instance, the tremendous struggles for liberation of the slaves of the French West Indies (especially St. Domingo or Haiti) in the 1790's and early 1800's certainly inspired similar attempts in the United States. It is to be noted, too, that attempts at revolt evoked more stringent measures of repression, and the added pinch these created was at times probably important in causing new conspiracies or rebellions.

The more rapid growth of the Negro population as compared to that of the white was also a disturbing factor. This occurred for various reasons. When, in the late seventeenth and early eighteenth centuries, Negro slavery was found to be profitable in certain regions, greed led to an enormous spurt in the importation of slaves. This undoubtedly is an explanation for the considerable slave unrest in South Carolina in the 1730's. The settlement of new and fertile slave areas was likewise followed by a disproportionate growth of the Negro population and consequent slave unrest, as in Mississippi in 1835. Depression, on the other hand, in the great staple producing areas caused them to import less slaves. This meant a severe blow to the prosperity of the slave-raising and slave-exporting regions of the South, with a resultant rapid rise in their slave populations and a more dangerous social condition. This state of affairs prevailed, for instance, from about 1820 to 1831 in eastern Virginia and eastern North Carolina.

Urbanization and industrialization—which were occurring to some extent in the South from about 1840 to 1860 —and their creation of a proletarian Negro were also exceedingly dangerous to a slave society. These phenomena were probably important in accounting for some slave outbreaks, especially those of the late 1850's.

SAFEGUARDS OF THE SLAVOCRATS

While the propaganda mill of the slavocratic oligarchy incessantly ground out its falsehoods concerning the innate cowardice and stupidity of the Negro and the delights of being a slave, the same group nevertheless maintained a whole series of devices and laws which it knew was necessary to keep the Negro in bondage.

Armed might was the main instrument of suppression. This comprised large detachments of regular troops of the United States Army, the efficient militia of each of the Southern states, the patrols or mounted bodies of armed men who scoured every piece of land in every county of the South at various intervals from one week to four weeks, the considerable bodies of guards present and active in every Southern city, volunteer military organizations in numerous areas of the South, and the continual presence of at least one armed white, master or overseer, on every plantation.

The activities of the slaves were severely limited. None might possess arms. It was illegal to teach a slave how to read or write. Writing or saying anything with a "tendency" to create unrest among the slaves was a serious crime. No slave might buy or sell or trade anything without his master's permission. Slaves might not assemble without the presence of whites. They could not testify in any court in any case involving whites. Legal restrictions also hit free Negroes, so that their movements from county to county or from state to state were regulated or totally forbidden. They, too, could not testify in any court against a white person. They, as a rule, could not vote, and even their business activities were closely regulated and limited. In the two years immediately preceding the Civil War laws were passed in several Southern states having as their purposes the re-enslavement of free Negroes or their forced evacuation.

Numerous non-legal regulations and customs were important, too, in maintaining subordination. The opinion of a North Carolina judge rendered in 1852 indicated some of these:

What acts in a slave towards a white person will amount to insolence, it is manifestly impossible to define—it may consist in a look, the pointing of a finger, a refusal or neglect to step out of the way when a white person is seen to approach. But each of such acts violates the rules of propriety, and if tolerated, would destroy that subordination, upon which our social system rests.

A carefully nursed policy of division between the poor whites and the slaves on the basis of race hatred was another very important Bourbon device for retaining his power. Divisions amongst the slaves themselves were also fostered. Thus the domestic slaves were, generally, better treated than the field slaves. It was from this favored group that the slaveholders recruited spies and traitors to whom they gave considerable financial rewards together, often, with freedom—the greatest gift in the power of the "patriarchal" slaveholders!

14

The slaveholders' religion had, so far as the slave was concerned, one message—be meek. In the words of the Rev. Dr. Nelson, who lived for many years in North Carolina:

I have been intimately acquainted with the religious opportunities of the slaves,—in the constant habit of hearing the sermons which are preached to them. And I solemnly affirm that, during the forty years of my residence and observation in this line, I never heard a single one of these sermons but what was taken up with the obligations and duties of slaves to their masters. Indeed, I never heard a sermon to slaves but what made obedience to masters by the slaves the fundamental and supreme law of religion.

But the slaves had a different religion. Their God had declared that all men were created of one blood, and that the divine rule of doing unto others as one would have others do unto you was the true guide for religious behavior. Their God had cursed man-stealers and had himself taken slaves out of their bondage. Their God had denounced the oppressors and had praised the humble. Their God had declared that the first would be last and the last would be first.

II. THE REVOLTS AND CONSPIRACIES

Before discussing the slave revolts themselves it is important that it be understood that they form but one manifestation of the discontent of the Negro. Revolt was merely one method by which the slaves hoped to obtain their liberty. There were others, each of which merits extensive treatment. One of the most important of these was flight. In the history of slavery many tens of thousands of slaves *succeeded* in escaping from their enslavers. They fled wherever freedom loomed—the destinations varying with the different times and places—to the Dutch, the Indians, the Mexicans, the British armies, the Canadians, the French, the Spanish, to the Northern states and to the swamps and mountains and forests of the South.

Other slaves, particularly those who were leased by their masters for work in towns and cities, were able, by working in their spare time, to accumulate enough money to purchase their freedom (this was possible, of course, only if the master were willing and honest). There is considerable evidence to indicate that this was by no means infrequent, especially in the more northern of the slave states, like Tennessee, Kentucky and Missouri.

Enlistment and faithful service in the armed forces of the nation was another method whereby Negroes at times gained their freedom. Several hundreds, for example, became free in this manner in the two wars against Great Britain. Individual acts of terrorism, self-mutilation and self-destruction (sometimes, as in Charleston, in 1807, mass suicides), sabotage, as shamming illness, "careless" work, destruction of tools and occasionally strikes were other forms of protest against enslavement.

It is, finally, not to be forgotten that Negroes were leaders in the agitational and political movement against slavery, none being more important in these respects than Allen, Jones, Hall, Truth, Purvis, Remond, Garnet, Ruggles, Wright, Still, Tubman, Walker, Ray, Douglass and a host of others.

THE EARLIEST REVOLTS

The first settlement within the present borders of the United States to contain Negro slaves was the victim of the first slave revolt. A Spanish colonizer, Lucas Vasquez de Ayllon, in the summer of 1526, founded a town near the mouth of the Pedee river in what is now South Carolina. The community consisted of five hundred Spaniards and one hundred Negro slaves. Trouble soon beset the colony. Illness caused numerous deaths, carrying off, in October, Ayllon himself. The Indians grew more hostile and dangerous. Finally, probably in November, the slaves rebelled, killed several of their masters, and escaped to the Indians. This was a fatal blow and the remaining colonists—but one hundred and fifty souls—returned to Haiti in December, 1526.

The first slave plots and revolts in English America did not occur until the latter half of the seventeenth century. This is due to the fact that very few Negroes were there until about 1680. Thus in 1649 Virginia contained but three hundred Negroes, and twenty-one years later the Negroes numbered but two thousand, or some five per cent of the total population. It is also to be noticed that Negroes were not legally enslaved until about 1660, and not enslaved by custom until about 1640. The only crop produced by relatively large-scale labor in the seventeenth century was tobacco, and this was mainly raised by white indentured servants until about 1675.

With the opening of the eighteenth century and the development of large-scale cultivation of rice and indigo as well as tobacco, Negro slavery became important, and frequent and serious revolts occurred. By 1715 about one-third the population of Virginia, the Carolinas and Maryland were slaves (46,000 out of 123,000). Within five years importation of slaves became important in Louisiana also. Georgia adopted slavery by 1750, and four years later the five English provinces of Georgia, the Carolinas, Virginia and Maryland contained a quarter of a million Negro slaves out of a total population of 609,000.

In September, 1663, a favorite servant of a Mr. John

17

Smith of Gloucester county, Virginia, betrayed an extensive conspiracy of Negro slaves and white indentured servants. An unknown number of the rebels was executed. The day of the betrayal was set aside by the colonists as one of thanksgiving and prayer to a merciful God who had saved them from extermination. The traitor was given his freedom and 5,000 pounds of tobacco.

There is evidence of several other slave plots in the seventeenth century, probably the most important of which was that of 1687 in Virginia. But, for the reasons made clear by the economic and population data already presented, the really serious uprisings do not occur until the early years of the next century. From that time until final emancipation, one hundred and sixty years later, the history of Negro slavery is filled with heroic and carefully planned mass plots or outbreaks.

It is manifestly impossible within the confines of this booklet to deal with each of these events, or even to exhaustively treat any of the main revolts. We shall, however, attempt to briefly describe the more important uprisings. (A complete list of plots and revolts will be found in the Appendix.)

1709-1730

A joint conspiracy of Negro and Indian slaves was uncovered and crushed in the counties of Surry and Isle of Wight, Virginia, in 1709. The court of investigation declared that "greate numbers" were involved. The next year another extensive conspiracy, this time only of Negro slaves, was again discovered in Surry county. A slave named Peter was the leader. Another slave, Will, was the traitor. His reward was freedom. South Carolina was greatly troubled by slave rebelliousness in 1711. According to the provincial legislature, this kept the inhabitants "in great fear and terror."

A serious uprising occurred in New York City in 1712. A contemporary declared that the plot was formed January 1, "the Conspirators tying themselves to secrecy by Sucking ye blood of each Others hands." Very early in the morning of April 8, about twenty-five Negro slaves set fire to a house, and then, with a few guns, clubs and knives ready, waited for the whites to approach. They did, and about nine were killed and seven severely wounded. The alarm soon spread and soldiers hastened to the disturbance. In about twenty-four hours most of the rebels were captured. Six, however, were not, for they committed suicide; "one shot first his wife and then himself and some who had hid themselves in Town when they went to Apprehend them Cut their own throats."

Twenty-one slaves were executed. According to the account of the Governor:

some were burnt others hanged, one broke on the wheele, and one hung a live in chains in the town, so that there has been the most exemplary punishment inflicted that could be possibly thought of.

This revolt was important in leading Massachusetts and Pennsylvania to pass effective tariff regulations to cut down the importation of slaves.

An extensive revolt occurred in the drought-stricken and Indian-menaced area of Charleston, S. C., in 1720. Precise numbers are unknown but many slaves were banished from the province, some hanged and others burned alive.

The summer of 1730 witnessed the suppression of three serious slave outbreaks, one in five counties of Virginia, centering in Williamsburg, one in Charleston, S. C., and one in Louisiana.

The unrest in Virginia seems to have been brewing for weeks prior to the main outbreak, for several suspected slaves were early arrested and lashed. Later, on a Sunday, two hundred slaves assembled and chose leaders for an insurrection planned for the near future. Betrayal came, however, and at least four of the leaders were executed. On October 28, 1730 it was ordered that henceforth, in Virginia, all who went to worship the Prince of Peace were to go armed.

Information concerning the Charleston plot of 1730 is far from statisfying, but it is certain that many Negroes were involved. Disagreement as to method among the slaves led to betrayal and the familiar report, "ringleaders executed." One contemporary letter states that "had not an overruling Providence discovered their Intrigues, we had all been in blood."

The unguarded speech of a slave woman who, on being beaten, shouted that Negroes would not be beaten much longer, led to investigation and the disclosure, after torture with fire, of a plot amongst the slaves of Louisiana, in 1730. The leader, Samba, had headed an uprising against whites in Africa and had been shipped to America. He and seven other men were "broke alive on the wheel," and one slave woman was hanged "before their eyes." Two years later the discovery of another plot here led to the hanging of another woman and the breaking of four more men on a wheel. As a further stimulus to contentment, the heads of the four men were strung on poles near the city of New Orleans. Incidentally, some idea of conditions in Louisiana at this time may be gained from the fact that though 7,000 slaves had been imported between 1719 and 1731, in the latter year there were less than 3,500 living.

1739-1741

There were three distinct uprisings in South Carolina in 1739. One of them, which took place in Charleston during March, involved a Spaniard and an Irishman, as well as slaves. The most serious, however, was that led by Cato. This started on a plantation at Stono, some twenty miles west of Charleston, on the ninth of September. The slaves killed the two guards of a magazine, armed themselves and set out for the Edisto river, to the west. Their aim was to escape into Spanish-held Florida, the Governor of which had promised liberty to all fugitive English slav ..

A contemporary wrote: "Several Negroes joyned them, they called out liberty, marched on with colours displayed, and two drums beating." They destroyed and burned everything in their path in this bid for freedom, so that, as an eye-witness said, "The Country thereabout was full of flames."

About thirty whites were killed, but not indiscriminately, for one—"a good man and kind to his slaves"—was spared. Scores of well-armed whites soon overtook the slaves, and in a surprise attack killed fourteen Negroes. In two more days of pursuit and battle twenty more rebels were killed and forty captured. These "were immediately some shot, some hang'd, and some Gibbeted alive." About twenty were yet at large and in another engagement, in which the slaves "fought stoutly for some time," ten more were killed. Apparently ten slaves made good their bid for freedom.

Early in June, 1740, a slave plot, involving at least two hundred Negroes in and about Charleston, was discovered a short time before it was to have matured. On the day set for the outbreak about one hundred and fifty Negroes had gathered but, while yet unarmed, they were surprised and attacked by the whites. Fifty were captured and hanged, ten a day. In this same month the city was swept by a terrific fire, doing well over a million pounds damage and necessitating aid from other colonies. This was at first ascribed to the slaves, but was later denied. The cause is not positively known, but it is certain that in the summer of 1741 at least two slaves were executed for incendiarism in Charleston.

It is this revolutionary activity, and the Negro's habit of running away, that were important considerations impelling statesmen conected with the settlement of Georgia, like Oglethorpe and Egmont, to prohibit Negroes in that colony. This prohibition lasted until 1749. South Carolina itself passed laws in 1740 for the purpose of lessening the danger. Slave importations were taxed, the funds raised to be used for obtaining white Protestant settlers. Rather vague regulations requiring better food and clothes for the slaves were passed. It was also most generously provided that a master was not to work his slave more than fourteen hours a day in the winter or more than fifteen hours a day in the summer!

The slave plot of 1741 in New York City has been dealt with by historians as either a complete frameup resulting from a baseless panic, or as a real and considerable conspiracy. The truth is probably somewhere between those two ideas. Discontent certainly was rife. England was at the moment waging an unpopular and costly war against Spain and New York itself, early in 1741, was momentarily expecting attack. Probably of more importance was the fact that the winter of 1740-41 was a particularly severe one, six feet of snow being common in the city. The suffering among the poor generally and the slaves especially was most acute.

Yet the star witness against the conspirators, Mary Burton, as her own testimony establishes, was a liar, and the methods used to extract confessions from the prisoners, torture or promises of rewards, militate against their com-plete acceptance.

Nevertheless, beginning in March there were a series of

suspicious fires and many contemporaries were convinced that some, at least, of these were set by Negro slaves and by white accomplices. Indeed, the Governor of the Province declared on June 20, "if the truth were ever known, there are not many innocent Negro men, and it is thought that some Negroes of the Country are accomplices and were ready to act there." This last idea undoubtedly arose from the fact that there were frequent and suspicious fires in Hackensack, New Jersey, for which at least two slaves were executed, by burning, on the fifth of May.

Whatever may be the facts as to the justification for the panic aroused among the slaveholders, the results of that panic are unquestionable. About one hundred and fifty slaves and twenty-five whites were arrested. Four whites and thirteen slaves were burned alive. Eighteen Negroes were hanged, two of them in chains, seven who were indicted were not captured, and about seventy were banished.

DURING THE FIRST AMERICAN REVOLUTION

Abigail, the honest and forthright wife of John Adams, wrote to her husband (himself, at the moment, leading a revolution) in September, 1774, of the discovery of a fairly widespread plot for rebellion among the slaves of Boston. And she closed in this fashion: "I wish most sincerely there was not a slave in the province; it always appeared a most iniquitous scheme to me to fight ourselves for what we are daily robbing and plundering from those who have as good a right to freedom as we have."

The revolutionary activity amongst the colonists certainly brought such ideas forcibly to the minds of the Negro slaves. The commotion enhanced the possibility of gaining freedom without, however, resorting to the desperate expedient of rebellion, and thousands of slaves grabbed the chance by flight and by enlistment in the opposing armies. It is also true that Mrs. Adams' sentiments were held by many other white people, amongst them slaveholders, so that the period of America's First Revolution witnessed hundreds of manumissions of slaves. These factors served as safety valves and cut down the number of plots and revolts. Nevertheless several occurred.

Probably the most important of these was that which rocked Pitt, Beaufort and Craven counties, North Carolina, in July, 1775. Two slaves betrayed the plot on the day set for the outbreak, the eighth of July. Immediately all was military activity. In Craven county alone forty slaves were arrested the first day and questioned before a citizens' committee who found "a deep laid Horrid Tragick Plan" for rebellion. For several days thereafter, throughout the counties mentioned, dozens of slaves were apprehended (some of whom were armed, and some killed resisting arrest). The favorite sentence seems to have been "to receive 80 lashes each [and] to have both Ears crap'd." Rather crude displays of "kindliness" to inflict upon people who, as Professor Phillips has stated, were "by racial quality submissive"!

1791-1802

The next period of serious organized disaffection among America's "docile" Negroes extended from 1791 through 1802. These years witnessed a remarkable conjunction of those types of events which were most conducive to slave unrest.

Economic distress was characteristic of the period throughout the South and was most acute in the regions of greatest unrest, Louisiana, North Carolina and Virginia. In the latter two states there was a considerable exodus of impoverished whites seeking better opportunities and this, together with a decline in the exportation of slaves, resulted in a much more rapid growth of the Negro population as compared with the white.

The period was also, of course, one of a great world-wide outburst of revolutionary activity. These were the years of the French Revolution, of the cry "liberty, equality, fraternity," slogans representing precisely those things of which the Negro people, more than any other, were deprived. The year 1791 marked the beginning of the revolution of the Negro slaves in St. Domingo, which, after fourteen years of unsurpassed heroism, culminated in the establishment of an independent Negro republic. Both events filled American newspapers and formed the great topic of conversation in the North and in the South. The latter event, the Negro revolution, directly affected the South, for it caused an exodus of thousands of panic-stricken slaveholders, together with some slaves, into cities like Richmond, Norfolk and Charleston.

The general upsurge of revolutionary feeling gave a considerable impetus to anti-slavery sentiment. In the South this resulted in the freeing of hundreds of slaves by conscience-stricken masters, the growth of anti-slavery groups like the Quakers and Methodists and, indeed, the formation of emancipationist societies in several of the more northern of the slave states. In the North the period was marked by the enactment of gradual emancipation acts so that by 1802 every Northern state (except New Jersey, whose act came in 1804) had provided for the ultimate extinction of slavery.

It is to be noted that even in this early period, the anti-slavery feeling went, in some cases, to the extent of condoning if not urging slave rebellion. This was true of a Boston writer, J. P. Martin, who declared, in 1791, that if the American Revolution was just, then surely a rebellion of slaves would be just. It was true of the Kentuckian, David Rice, who in that state's constitutional convention of 1792 declared that the slaves of St. Domingo were "engaged in a noble conflict." It was true of a prominent citizen of Connecticut, Theodore Dwight, who published his sentiments in 1794. Similar ideas appeared in Northern newspapers of these years, and a Massachusetts Negro leader, Prince Hall, suggested, in 1797, that American Negroes would do well to imitate those of the French West Indies.

Finally, this was the period, beginning about 1795, of the spread of two great staple crops, sugar and cotton, due to the inventions of Boré and Whitney. It was, then, a period of extremely rapid transformation in the economic life of the South. It was a time of the very greatly increased commercialization of slavery. Slavery became more than ever before the foundation of a "big business," a heartless big business whose markets were unlimited and whose workers were completely in the power of the bosses. These laborers represented, indeed, the system's greatest investment, and that investment had to yield profits no matter what it meant in sweat and blood and tears.

Slave uprisings occurred in lower Louisiana in 1791 and in 1792. Details, however, are unknown. The latter year also witnessed very serious trouble during May, June and July, in Norfolk, Portsmouth, Hampton and the counties of Northampton, Greenbrier and Kanawha in Virginia, as well as in the neighborhood of Newbern, North Carolina. Many hundreds of slaves were implicated, scores were jailed, dozens lashed and several executed. There were sporadic attacks on whites, especially on patrols. Clubs, spears and some guns were found in the possession of slaves.

A Mr. Randolph of Richmond overheard three slaves, on the night of July 20, 1793, discussing plans for a forthcoming revolt and even allocating the property they were to seize. "The one who seemed to be the chief speaker said, you see how the blacks has killed the whites in the French Island [St. Domingo] and took it a while ago." Other people, including John Marshall, Chief Justice of the Supreme Court of the United States, reported, as late as November 25, discoveries of plots in Petersburg, Portsmouth, Elizabeth City, and in Powhatan and Warwick counties, Virginia. The familiar story was repeated: mobilization and arming of the militias of the affected areas, the arrest of scores of slaves and the torture and execution of the rebel leaders.

The next major outbreak occurred in 1795 in Pointe Coupée parish in the (then) Spanish colony of Louisiana. The conspiracy was betrayed after disagreement among the leaders as to when to revolt. The militia was immediately armed, and with the aid of regular soldiers the plot was crushed. The slaves resisted arrest, and twenty-five of them were killed. Twenty-three others were executed, and the bodies of nine of these were left hanging near the churches of the region. Many others were severely lashed. It appears certain that at least three whites were implicated with the slaves and were banished from the colony. There is, also, evidence of a slave conspiracy in May of this year in St Landry parish, Louisiana. A direct result of this rebellious activity in Spanish Louisiana was the banning of the slave trade.

Two months later the depredations of a group of outlawed runaway slaves and the killing of an overseer, led to an intense slave hunt in New Hanover county, North Carolina. At least four of these black Robin Hoods were captured and executed.

GABRIEL'S CONSPIRACY

The year 1800 is the most important one in the history of American Negro slave revolts. For it is the birth year of John Brown and of Nat Turner, the year in which Denmark Vesey bought his freedom, and it is the year of the great Gabriel conspiracy.

It is clear that this conspiracy, under the leadership of Gabriel, slave of Thomas Prosser, and of Jack Bowler, another slave (both of Henrico county, Virginia), was well formed by the spring of 1800. Apparently wind of this early reached the authorities, for Virginia's Governor, James Monroe, expressed "fears of a negro insurrection" as early as April 22. Yet, as a contemporary declared, the plot was "kept with incredible Secrecy for several months," and it was not until August 9 that Monroe was warned, in a letter from Petersburg, of a forthcoming revolt. The military authorities were instantly informed of this.

The next disclosure came in the afternoon of the day, Saturday, August 30, set for the outbreak. It was made by Mr. Mosby Sheppard, whose two slaves, Tom and, aptly enough, Pharaoh, had told him of the plot. Monroe acted immediately. He appointed three aides for himself, asked for and got the use of the federal armory at Manchester, posted cannon at the capitol, called into service at least six hundred and fifty troops, and gave notice of the conspiracy to every militia commander in the state.

"But," as an eyewitness declared, "upon that very evening just about Sunset, there came on the most terrible thunder, accompanied with an enormous rain, that I ever witnessed in this State." This storm flooded rivers and tore down bridges and made military activity for both the rebels and the slaveholders impossible. A patrol captain did, however, report observing an exodus of slaves out of Richmond, whereas, usually, on Saturdays, the slaves from the countryside flocked into the town.

As a matter of fact on that stormy night at least one thousand slaves had appeared at their agreed rendezvous, six miles outside of Richmond, armed with clubs and swords; but after vainly trying to advance in the face of the flood, the rebels dispersed.

The next day scores of slaves were arrested. About thirty-five Negroes were executed. At least four condemned slaves escaped from prison, and at least one committed suicide. The leader, Gabriel, a twenty-four year old giant of six feet two, was finally captured in Norfolk on September 25 and sent to Richmond. He was tried and condemned, but his execution was postponed for three days, until October 7, in the hope that he would talk. Monroe himself interviewed him, but reported that, "From what he said to me, he seemed to have made up his mind to die, and to have resolved to say but little on the subject of the conspiracy."

Thomas Jefferson pointed out to Monroe that the "other states & the world at large will forever condemn us if we indulge a principle of revenge, or go one step beyond absolute necessity. They cannot lose sight of the rights of the two parties, & the object of the unsuccessful one." Ten condemned slaves were reprieved and banished.

Certain features of this conspiracy merit special attention. It is certain that the motivating drive of the rebels, as one of their leaders said, was "death or liberty." This spirit is also shown by their heroic behavior before the courts and the gallows of the slavocrats. John Randolph, who attended the trials, declared that the slaves "manifested a sense of their rights, and contempt of danger, and a thirst for revenge which portend the most unhappy circumstances." Another lawyer who was present at the trials told an English visitor, Robert Sutcliff, of the courageous actions of the slaves. He declared that when one of the Negroes was asked,

29

what he had to say to the court in his defense, he replied, in a manly tone of voice, "I have nothing more to offer than what General Washington would have had to offer, had he been taken by the British officers and put to trial by them. I have ventured my life in endeavouring to obtain the liberty of my countrymen, and am a willing sacrifice to their cause; and I beg, as a favour, that I may be immediately led to execution. I know that you have pre-determined to shed my blood, why then all this mockery of a trial?"

And a resident of Richmond wrote, September 9, 1800: "Of those who have been executed, no one has betrayed his cause. They have uniformly met death with fortitude."

It was this love of liberty which led the slaves to plan no harm to anti-slavery groups like the Methodists and the Quakers. The French inhabitants were also to be exempt from attack, for they personified to the slaves the ideals of liberty and equality. Poor white women were also in no case to be injured. The slaves expected too, or at least hoped that the poorer whites would join them in their struggle against the slaveholders. They counted, too, on the aid of the nearby Catawba Indians. Testimony offered at the trials directly implicated two Frenchmen, but they were never named and never captured.

It is not known how many slaves were involved in the conspiracy. One witness said 2,000, one 5,000 and one 10,000. The Governor of Mississippi thought 50,000 were implicated. Monroe himself said:

It was distinctly seen that it embraced most of the slaves in this city [Richmond] and neighbourhood, and that the combination extended to several of the adjacent counties, Hanover, Caroline, Louisa, Chesterfield, and to the neighbourhood of the Point of the Fork; [Columbia in Goochland county was known as Point of the Fork]—there was good cause to believe that the knowledge of such a project pervaded other parts, if not the whole of the State.

(In 1800 there were about 347,000 slaves in Virginia. In the regions specified by Monroe there were about 32,000 slaves.)

Serious unrest came to the surface again in 1802. Indeed, plots had been uncovered in Norfolk just three months after Gabriel's capture, and again in the winter of 1801 in Petersburg. On January 2, 1802, trouble was once more reported from Petersburg and the militia was pressed into service. Five days later two slave conspirators were sentenced to death in Nottoway county, Virginia.

A letter of January 18 from a Negro to another in Powhatan referred to a plot and declared, "Our travelling friend has got ten thousand in readiness for the night." Two slaves were hanged in Brunswick on February 12 (seven years, to the day, before Abe Lincoln saw the light). Two more were executed in April in Halifax, and many arrests were then reported from Princess Anne and Norfolk. A rebel was executed in the latter city in May. The editor of the Norfolk *Herald* thought this conspiracy was more widespread than that of 1800. Fears in Virginia were increased when, in May, plots were reported from North Carolina.

The trouble there was widespread, conspiracies being uncovered in the counties of Camden, Currituck, Bertie, Martin, Pasquotank, Halifax, Warren, Washington, Wake and Charlotte. Hundreds of slaves were arrested, scores lashed, branded and cropped, and about fifteen hanged. The finding of pikes and swords amongst the slaves was several times mentioned. Six Negroes, "mounted on horseback," attacked the jail in Elizabeth City with the aim of rescuing their imprisoned comrades, but their attempt was defeated and four of them were captured. It appears that the leader of the North Carolina rebels was named Tom Copper and that he, with several followers, had been fugitive slaves for months.

There is good evidence that white people were accomplices of the slaves in the Virginia plots of 1802. Thus a Mr. John Scott, while informing the Governor of the trial and execution of slaves in Halifax, stated, "I have just received information that three white persons were concerned in the plot; that they have arms and ammunition concealed under their houses, and were to give aid when the negroes should begin." A slave, Lewis, twice stated at his trial that whites, "that is, the common run of poor white people," were involved. And Arthur Farrar, a slave leader, appealed for support from his fellow slaves with these words:

Black men if you have now a mind to join with me now is your time for freedom. All clever men who will keep secret these words I give to you is life. I have taken it on myself to let the country be at liberty this lies upon my mind for a long time. Mind men I have told you a great deal I have joined with both black and white which is the common man or poor white people, mulattoes will join with me to help free the country, although they are free already. I have got 8 or 10 white men to lead me in the fight on the magazine, they will be before me and hand out the guns, powder, pistols, shot and other things that will answer the purpose... black men I mean to lose my life in this way if they will take it.

Arthur was hanged in Henrico county on June 18, 1802.

1810-1816

The years 1810-1816 mark the next period of serious concerted slave unrest. Here again the familiar pattern of surrounding conditions is apparent. Severe depression, due to soil exhaustion, to the non-intercourse and embargo acts passed prior to the War of 1812, and the blockade and devastation brought by that war caused acute suffering in the slave states. The excitement incident to the waging of the war itself also affected the slaves.

There were other military events of the period affecting the slave areas, as the revolution in and American annexation of West Florida in 1810, and the slavocratic filibusters from 1811 to 1813, and again in 1816 against Texas and East Florida. Revolutionary struggles in Mexico and in South America (Simon Bolivar started his career in 1810) filled American newspapers. The antislavery activity of Bolivar (which was fostered by his Negro ally, Alexandre Petion, President of Haiti) was especially alarming to and anxiously discussed by the rulers of the slave states.

In March, 1810, two communications were found on a road in Halifax county, North Carolina. One was from a slave in Greene county, Georgia, to another slave, Cornell Lucas, of Martin county, N. C.; another, likewise to and from slaves, had been sent from Tennessee and was intended for Brunswick county, Virginia. The contents of both letters, even as to details, were similar, and one, that to Cornell Lucas, may be quoted in full:

Dear Sir—I received your letter to the fourteenth of June, 1809, with great freedom and joy to hear and understand what great proceedance you have made, and the resolution you have in proceeding on in business as we have undertook, and hope you will still continue in the same mind. We have spread the sense nearly over the continent in our part of the country, and have the day when we are to fall to work, and you must be sure not to fail on that day, and that is the 22d April, to begin about midnight, and do the work at home first, and then take the armes of them you slay first, and that will strengthen us more in armes—for freedom we want and will have, for we have served this cruel land long enuff, & be as secret convaing your nuse as possabel, and be sure to send it by some cearfull hand, and if it happens to be discovered, fail not in the day, for we are full abel to conquer

33

by any means.—Sir, I am your Captain James, living in the state of Jorgy, in Green county—so no more at present, but remaining your sincer friend and captain until death.

General Thomas Blount, a North Carolina Congressman, informed the Governor of Georgia of these letters. This probably explains the passage in the latter's legislative message referring to information he had received "from a source so respectable as to admit but little doubt of the existence of a plan of an insurrection being formed among our domesticks and particularly in Greene county." A resident in Augusta, Georgia (about fifty miles east of Greene county) wrote to a friend April 9, 1810:

The letter from "Captain James" is but a small part of the evidence of the disposition of the Blacks in this part of the country. The most vigorous measures are taking to defeat their infernal designs. May God preserve us from the fate of St. Domingo. The papers here will, for obvious reasons, observe a total silence on this business; and the mail being near closing, I can say no more on the subject at present.

And so far as Georgia is concerned "no more on the subject" is known.

A letter of May 30, 1810, from a Virginia slaveholder, Richard W. Byrd of Smithfield, to the Governor, John Tyler, told of the discovery of insurrectionary schemes among the slaves of his neighborhood and of North Carolina. Many were arrested and lashed. Slave preachers, especially one named Peter, were declared to be the leading rebels. One had declared that "he was entitled to his freedom, and he would be damned, if he did not have it in a fortnight." Early in June at least one slave, Sam, of Isle of Wight, and two others, Glasgow and Charlotte, of Culpeper, were found guilty of conspiracy. The woman was lashed, Sam was banished and Glasgow was executed. At the same time trouble was reported from Norfolk, but details are not known.

At the end of November, 1810, "a dangerous conspiracy among the negroes was discovered" in Lexington, Kentucky. "A great many Negroes were put in jail," according to a resident, but what became of them is not reported.

On the afternoon of January 9, 1811, the people of New Orleans were thrown into the "utmost dismay and confusion" on discovering wagons and carts, straggling into the city, filled with people whose faces "wore the masks of consternation" and who told of having just escaped from "a miniature representation of the horrors of St. Domingo." They had fled from a revolt of slaves, numbering about four hundred, of St. Charles and St. John the Baptist parishes, about thirty-five miles away from the city. These slaves, led by Charles Deslondes, described as a "free mulatto from St. Domingo," rose on the evening of January 8, starting at the plantation of a Major Andry.

They were originally armed with cane knives, axes and clubs. After killing Andry's son and wounding the Major, they took possession of a few guns, drums and some sort of flags, and started marching from plantation to plantation, slaves everywhere joining them. They killed at least one other white man and destroyed a few plantations.

Major Andry, according to his own statement, organized about eighty well-armed planters and, on the ninth of January, attacked the slaves, "of whom we made great slaughter." Many, however, escaped this first attack and continued their depredations. Andry ordered "several strong detachments to pursue them through the woods, and," he wrote on January 11, "at every moment our men bring in or kill them."

Meanwhile, in New Orleans, Governor Claiborne had, on January 9, appointed seven aides for himself, called out the militia and forbidden male Negroes from going at large. Brigadier-General Wade Hampton immediately left that city with four hundred militiamen and sixty United

States Army men for the scene of action. Major Milton left Baton Rouge at about the same time with two hundred more soldiers.

These forces, very early in the morning of the tenth, attacked the rebellious slaves and decimated them. Sixty-six were killed or executed on the spot, sixteen were captured and sent to New Orleans, and seventeen were reported as missing and were "supposed generally to be dead in the woods, as many bodies have been seen by the patrols." All those tried in New Orleans were executed, at least one, a leader named Gilbert, by the firing squad; and their heads were strung at intervals from the city to Andry's plantation. Hampton reported on January 12 that Milton had been for the time being posted in the neighborhood to aid "various companies of the citizens, that are scouring the country in every direction." At the same time a company of light artillery and one of dragoons were sent up the river to suppress "disturbances that may have taken place higher up."

Governor Claiborne, writing January 19, said he was "happy to find . . . so few Slaves are now in the woods. I hope this dreadful Insurrection is at an end and I pray God! we may never see another." What else occurred cannot be said, but this paragraph from a Louisiana paper is suggestive:

We are sorry to learn that a ferocious sanguinary disposition marked the character of some of the inhabitants. Civilized man ought to remember well his standing, and never let himself sink down to a level with the savage; our laws are summary enough and let them govern.

A law of April 25, 1811, provided for the payment by the Territory of twenty-nine thousand dollars as some compensation to the masters whose slaves were killed.

Repeatedly plots were uncovered and crushed during

the War of 1812. Those of most interest occurred in Louisiana in 1812 and in South Carolina in 1813.

In New Orleans, August 18, 1812, "it was discovered that an insurrection among the negroes was intended." The militia was immediately ordered out and was kept in service until the end of the month. White men and free Negroes were implicated with the slaves. One of these white men, Joseph Wood, was executed on September 13. "All the militia of the city were under arms—strong patrols were detailed for the night." It is clear that another of the whites involved in this plot was named Macarty, and that he was jailed, but what became of him or of the slave rebels, is not known.

There is evidence of unrest among the slaves of South Carolina in 1812 and of the existence of a widespread secret slave society there in 1813. The members of this group waited, vainly, for British aid to afford an opportunity to effectively strike for freedom. A song, said to have been written by a slave, and sung by these conspirators at their meetings, has been preserved. Its last stanza and chorus are:

> Arise! arise! shake off your chains!
> Your cause is just, so Heaven ordains;
> To you shall freedom be proclaimed!
> Raise your arms and bare your breasts,
> Almighty God will do the rest.
> Blow the clarion's warlike blast;
> Call every Negro from his task;
> Wrest the scourge from Buckra's hand,
> And drive each tyrant from the land!

> *Chorus:* Firm, united let us be,
> Resolved on death or liberty!
> As a band of patriots joined,
> Peace and plenty we shall find.

Early in 1816 Virginia was rocked by an indigenous John Brown, one George Boxley. In appearance he was anything but like Brown, but in ideas the two men were well nigh identical. Boxley was about thirty-five years old, six feet two inches tall, with a "thin visage, of a sallow complexion, thin make, his hair light or yellowish (thin on top of his head, and tied behind)—he stoops a little in his shoulders, has large whiskers, blue or grey eyes, pretends to be very religious, is fond of talking and speaks quick." Contemporaries were in doubt as to "whether he is insane or not," since he openly "declared that the distinction between rich and poor was too great; that offices were given rather to wealth than to merit; and seemed to be an advocate for a more leveling system of government. For many years he had avowed his disapprobation of the slavery of the Negroes, and wished they were free." It was believed that his failure to be elected to the state legislature sometime prior to the War of 1812, his declining economic fortunes, and his failure to advance in position while fighting in that war had embittered him.

Be that as it may, late in 1815 George Boxley decided to attempt to free the slaves and formed a conspiracy in Spotsylvania, Louisa and Orange counties. A slave woman betrayed it, and early in 1816 about thirty slaves were arrested. Boxley, after vainly trying to organize a rescue party, fled. He finally surrendered and was imprisoned but, with the flame of a candle and a file smuggled to him by his wife, he escaped, in May. Though a reward of one thousand dollars was offered for him he was never captured. About six slaves were hanged and the same number banished.

A favorite, but unnamed, slave betrayed a plot involving many Negroes in and around Camden, South Carolina, one month after Boxley's escape. The fourth of July was the day selected for the outbreak, which was to have been started by setting fire to several houses. Espionage was used to uncover the ramifications of this widespread conspiracy. A letter from Camden, dated July 4, stated that the slaves had been plotting since December, 1815, and that the local jail "is filled with negroes. They are stretched on their backs on the bare floor, and scarcely move their heads; but have a strong guard placed over them. . . . The negroes will never know who betrayed them, for they tried to engage all for a great distance round."

The legislature purchased, for one thousand one hundred dollars, the freedom of the traitor and passed a law giving him fifty dollars a year for the rest of his life. At least six rebel leaders were hanged.

Two major expeditions were carried out in 1816 against large settlements of outlawed fugitive slaves, one in South Carolina, the other in Florida. The maroons were attacked in the first case by the state militia, and in the second by infantry and artillery units of the regular United States army. About three hundred Negroes and a few whites were killed in these engagements.

1821-1831

From 1821 through 1831 there were incessant reports of slave unrest throughout the South. And, once more, that decade was marked by severe economic depression. Suffering was increased, too, by natural calamities such as drought in the southeast in 1826, in the southwest in 1827 and again in the southeast in 1830. Excessive rains ruined crops in South Carolina and Louisiana in 1829. Because of this depression there was a much more rapid increase of the slave population than the white population in the eastern slave states.

Revolutionary sentiments and slogans were in the air, and Southern papers were filled with praise for revolutionists in Turkey, Greece, Italy, Spain, France, Belgium, Poland, South America, the West Indies and Mexico. (It was only home-grown rebels who were referred to as "banditti" by the local press.) Slave uprisings in Brazil, Venezuela, Martinique, Puerto Rico, Cuba, Antigua, Tortola and Jamaica also found their way into the local press and conversation. The decade witnessed, too, an upsurge in the anti-slavery movement in England (which freed her colonial slaves in 1833), in Mexico (which abolished slavery in 1829), and in the border slave states and the northern states of America.

The activities of large numbers of outlawed fugitive slaves, aided by free Negroes, assumed the proportions of rebellion in the summer of 1821 in Onslow, Carteret and Bladen counties, North Carolina. There were, too, plans for joint action between these maroons and the field slaves against the slaveholders.

Approximately three hundred members of the militia of the three counties saw service for about twenty-five days in August and September. About twelve of these men were wounded when two companies accidentally fired upon each other. The situation was under control by the middle of September, and although the militia "did not succeed in apprehending all the runaways & fugitives, they did good by arresting some, and driving others off, and suppressing the spirit of insurrection." A newspaper report of May, 1824, disclosed that the "prime mover" of this trouble, Isam, "alias General Jackson," was among those who escaped at the time, for he is there reported as dying from lashes publicly inflicted at Cape Fear, North Carolina.

DENMARK VESEY

The conspiracy in and around Charleston, S. C., of 1822 was one of the most, if not the most, extensive in

American history. It was led by a former slave, Denmark Vesey, who had purchased his freedom in 1800.

Vesey, like most of the other rebels, was deeply religious. In justifying his plans to his numerous followers he read to them "from the bible how *the children of Israel were delivered out of Egypt from bondage.*" Antislavery speeches uttered in Congress during the Missouri debates of 1820-21 were also known to and encouraged the conspirators.

If Vesey's companion were to bow "to a white person he would rebuke him, and observe that all men were born equal, and that he was surprised that any one would degrade himself by such conduct; that he would never cringe to the whites, nor ought any who had the feelings of a man." He had not heeded the urgings of the slaveowners that free Negroes go to Africa, "*because he had not the will, he wanted to stay and see what he could do* for his fellow-creatures," including his own children, who were slaves. (These quotations are from the official record of the trials and all emphases are as in the original.)

Most of the other Negroes felt as Vesey did. Two of the rebels told a slaveholders' court, "They never spoke to any person of color on the subject, or knew of any one who had been spoken to by the other leaders, who had withheld his assent." Nevertheless, the leaders feared betrayal, and it came. One of them, Peter Poyas, had warned an agent, "Take care and don't mention it to those waiting men who receive presents of old coats, etc., from their masters, or they'll betray us." The traitor was Devany, favorite slave of Colonel Prioleau.

Vesey had picked the second Sunday in July as the day to revolt. Sunday was selected because on that day it was customary for slaves to enter the city, and July because many whites would then be away. The betrayal led him to put the date ahead one month, but Vesey could not communicate this to his country confederates, some of whom were eighty miles outside the city. Peter Poyas and Mingo Harth, the two leaders first arrested, behaved "with so much composure and coolness" that "the wardens were completely deceived." Both were freed on May 31, but spies were put on their trails. Another slave, William, gave further testimony and more arrests were made. The most damaging of these was the arrest of Charles Drayton, who agreed to act as a spy. This led to complete exposure.

One hundred and thirty-one Negroes were arrested in Charleston, and forty-seven condemned. Twelve were pardoned and transported, but thirty-five were hanged. Twenty were banished and twenty-six acquitted, although the owners were asked to transport eleven of these out of the state. Thirty-eight were discharged by the court. Four white men, American, Scottish, Spanish and German, were fined and imprisoned for aiding the Negroes by words of encouragement.

Although the leaders had kept lists of their comrades, only one list and part of another were found. Moreover, most of the executed slaves followed the advice of Poyas, "Die silent, as you shall see me do," and so it is difficult to say how many Negroes were involved. One witness said 6,600 outside of Charleston, and another said 9,000 altogether were implicated. The plan of revolt, comprising simultaneous attacks from five points and a sixth force on horseback to patrol the streets, further indicated a very considerable number of rebels.

The preparations had been thorough. By the middle of June the Negroes had made about two hundred and fifty pike heads and bayonets and over three hundred daggers. They had noted every store containing arms and had given instructions to all slaves who tended or could easily get horses as to when and where to bring the animals. Even a barber had assisted by making wigs as a disguise for the slaves. Vesey had also written twice to St. Domingo, telling of his plans and asking for aid.

After the arrests of the leaders many of the slaves planned their rescue, and an attempt to revolt in the city was suppressed by state troops. It was felt necessary to bring in Federal troops during the time of the executions.

There was trouble outside Charleston in July. Early that month three slaves were executed in Jacksonboro, forty miles west of the city. In August the Governor offered a reward of two hundred dollars for the arrest or killing of about twenty armed Negroes harassing the planters. In September a guarded report came of the discovery and crushing of a slave plot in Beaufort, S. C.; "The Town council was in secret session. Particulars had not transpired." They rarely did. Tighten restrictive laws, get rid of as many free Negroes as possible, keep the slaves ignorant, and your powder dry, hang the leaders, banish others, whip, crop, scourge scores, and above all keep it quiet, or, if you must talk, speak of the slaves' "contentedness" and "docility"!

The Norfolk *Herald* of May 12, 1823, under the heading "A Serious Subject," called attention to the activities, reaching revolt, of a growing number of pugnacious outlawed slaves in the southern part of Norfolk county, Virginia. The citizens of the region were in "a state of mind peculiarly harrassing and painful," for no one's life or property was secure. The Negroes had already obtained arms and had killed several slaveholders and overseers. Indeed, one slaveholder had received a note from these amazing men suggesting it would be healthier for him to remain indoors at night—and he did.

A large body of militia was ordered out to exterminate these outcasts and "thus relieve the neighbouring inhabitants from a state of perpetual anxiety and apprehension,

43

than which nothing can be more painful." During the next few weeks there were occasional reports of the killing or capturing of outlaws, culminating June 25 in the capture of the leader, Bob Ferebee. It was declared that he had been an outlaw for six years. Bob Ferebee was executed on the twenty-fifth of July.

The inhabitants of Edgecombe county, North Carolina, were much distraught in December, 1825, "by the partial discovery of an insurrectionary plot among the blacks." The slaves seem to have believed that the national government had set them free. The patrol was strengthened, the militia called out and the unrest crushed; but what that meant in human terms is not known.

Early in September, 1826, seventy-five slaves—chained on a slave-ship going down the Mississippi, with the boat one hundred miles south of Lexington, Kentucky—in some way broke their chains, killed their four guards and another white passenger and managed to get into Indiana. All the rebels "except one or two" were captured, five were hanged, some banished from the country and the rest sold south. The same year, twenty-nine slaves on board the domestic slave-ship, *Decatur,* revolted, killed the captain and mate, and commanded another white to take them to Haiti. The boat was captured and taken into New York, where in some way every one of the slaves escaped. One, however, William Bowser, was later captured and executed in New York City on December 15, 1826.

A lady in Georgia wrote, in June, 1827, that a "most dangerous and extensive insurrection of the blacks was detected at Macon a few days since." Three hundred slaves and one white man were involved, but no further particulars are known. Later that same month came the report of the destruction of a considerable group of slave outlaws in Alabama. These maroons had been exceedingly troublesome and were constantly gaining new recruits. They planned to build a fort just prior to their annihilation, and then "a great number of Negroes in the secret were to join them." In the attack, during which the Negroes "fought desperately" with what poor weapons they had, three slaves were killed, several escaped, and others were wounded and captured. One white was wounded.

The years 1829 and 1830 were filled with rebellious activities. Space permits but the barest mention of the outstanding events. Large-scale slave incendiarism was common, most notably in Augusta and Savannah, Georgia, in 1829, and in New Orleans and Cambridge, Maryland, in 1830. But, of course, the slaves did not restrict themselves to fire.

In February, 1829, slaves of several plantations forty miles north of New Orleans revolted. Militia suppressed the outbreak. At least two of the leaders were hanged. The Secretary of War wrote to the local commanding officer, Colonel Clinch, on March 17, 1829, to hold himself ready to aid the Governor of Louisiana, "on account of the insurrectionary spirit manifested by the black population in that state."

Probably in this same month a widespread conspiracy was uncovered in the neighborhood of Georgetown, South Carolina. The militia of the region was reinforced by troops and arms forwarded from Charleston. That the trouble was serious becomes clear from a letter of April 17, sent by the Attorney-General of the state to the military commander, General Allston, on the scene. The official comments that while the proceedings were not yet "bloody" he feared the General would "hang half the country. You must take care and save negroes enough for the rice crop." The leaders of this plot, all slaves, were Charles Prioleau, Nat, Robert and Quico. Quico was banished. What became of the others is not known.

The agitation of western Virginia for a greater share in the governing of the state, which was accompanied by much talk about liberty and equality, culminated in the constitutional convention of 1829-30. The excitement affected the slaves and inspired them to concerted efforts for freedom. Alarm pervaded Richmond, and the counties of Mathews, Isle of Wight, Gloucester and Hanover. Fears were intensified with the report of the killing of one white and the wounding of another in Hanover county on July 4, 1829, by about eight slaves. Patrols, militia and volunteer military bodies were pressed into service and crushed, for the time being, the "spirit of dissatisfaction and insubordination," to quote the Governor of Virginia.

In August, 1829, a drove of sixty slaves, men and women, were marching on their way to be sold in the deep South when, between Greenup and Vanceburg, Kentucky, two of the slaves apparently began to fight with each other. One of the white drivers came at them with a whip, and immediately all the slaves dropped their filed chains. Two of the white drivers were killed, but a third, with the aid of a slave woman, succeeded in escaping and obtained assistance; all the slaves were soon captured. What became of them is not known.

The same county in Kentucky, Greenup, witnessed, early in December, the execution of four slaves who had rebelled while being sent south and had killed their master. According to Southern newspapers the slaves "all maintained to the last, the utmost firmness and resignation to their fate. They severally addressed the assembled multitude, in which they attempted to justify the deed they had committed." One of the condemned slaves, the instant before being launched into eternity shouted, "death—death at any time in preference to slavery."

By this same month of December, 1829, copies of the

46

revolutionary pamphlet denouncing slavery, written by a free Negro of Boston, David Walker (and first published in September) were found amongst slaves and some whites in Louisiana, Georgia, North Carolina and Virginia. This evoked tremendous fear and led to increased police and military measures. It also definitely seems to have inspired slave plots, particularly in Wilmington, North Carolina, in September, 1830.

Going back, however, to December, 1829, we find that Negroes aboard the domestic slave-trader, *Lafayette*(!), bound for sale at New Orleans from Norfolk, revolted, with the aim of reaching St. Domingo. The slaves stated that a similar effort was to be made by Negroes on another boat from the same port. The slaves "were subdued, after considerable difficulty, and twenty-five of them were bolted down to the deck, until the arrival of the vessel at New Orleans."

Early in April, 1830, a conspiracy was uncovered in New Orleans, and at least two slaves were hanged. Plots were discovered in and around Dorchester, Maryland, in July. In October a conspiracy involving at least one hundred Negroes, including some who were free, was crushed in Plaquemines parish, Louisiana, by the local militia. In November plots were reported from Nashville, Tennessee, and from Wilmington, North Carolina.

On December 14, 1830, the inhabitants of Sampson, Bladen, New Hanover, and Duplin counties, North Carolina, petitioned the legislature for aid because their "slaves are become almost uncontroulable." Ten days later the residents of Newbern, Tarborough and Hillsborough in the same state were terrified by slave unrest. And "the inhabitants of Newbern being advised of the assemblage of sixty armed slaves in a swamp in their vicinity, the military were called out, and surrounding the swamp, killed the whole number." A resident of Wilmington, N. C.,

47

reported, on January 7, 1831, that: "There has been much shooting of negroes in this neighborhood recently, in consequence of symptoms of liberty having been discovered among them. These inhuman acts are kept profoundly secret." In Mississippi, too, on the day, in 1830, of the birth of the humble Prince of Peace, slave conspiracies were reported, particularly in Jefferson county.

The disaffection and unrest continued into the early months of 1831. Because of this and at the urgent requests of local authorities, the United States government sent two companies of infantry to New Orleans, and five more companies to Fort Monroe, in Virginia.

NAT TURNER

The terror prevalent in the South due to this rebellious activity was soon transformed into hysteria as the result of the actions of a slave named Nat Turner. He had been born October 2, 1800, and lived all his life in Southampton county, Virginia. When, in August, 1831, he led a rebellion, he was officially described as follows:

5 feet 6 or 8 inches high, weighs between 150 and 160 pounds, rather bright complexion, but not a mulatto, broad shoulders, large flat nose, large eyes, broad flat feet, rather knock-kneed, walks brisk and active, hair on the top of the head very thin, no beard, except on the upper lip and the top of the chin, a scar on one of his temples, also one on the back of his neck, a large knot on one of the bones of his right arm, near the wrist, produced by a blow.

Nat Turner was an intelligent and gifted man who could not reconcile himself to life as a slave. His religion offered him a rationalization for his rebellious feeling and, having taught himself how to read, he immersed himself in the stories of the Bible. His personality and keen mentality made him influential among his fellow-slaves and even with some neighboring poor whites.

In 1826 or 1827 he ran away, as his father had done successfully, and stayed away one month. Yet doubts overwhelmed him, and he felt that perhaps he "should return to the service of my earthly master." He did, but the other slaves "found fault, and murmured against me, saying that if they had my sense they would not serve any master in the world." In the spring of 1828 Turner, while working the fields, was finally convinced that he was to take up Christ's struggle for the liberation of the oppressed, "for the time was fast approaching when the first should be last and the last should be first."

The solar eclipse of February 12, 1831, was his sign. This fact has led chauvinistic historians to ridicule the "negro intelligence" (whatever that may mean) of Turner. The fact is that his (what would today be called) superstitious nature was common in his day among all people. Southerners still, generally, carried on agriculture according to the signs of the Zodiac. In 1833 under William Miller, a white citizen of New York, thousands of people were to be firmly convinced that the end of the world and the second coming of Christ were just around the corner. Indeed, that eclipse of 1831 itself led a white minister in New York City to prophesy that the whole city "South of Canal-Street would sink," and some folks actually moved to the upper part of the city.

Following the eclipse, Turner told four slaves it was time to prepare for rebellion. Significantly they selected July 4 as the day on which to strike for freedom. But Turner was ill on that day and he waited for another sign. This came on August 13 in the peculiar greenish blue color of the sun. A meeting was called for Sunday, August 21.

Turner arrived last and noticed a newcomer.

49

I saluted them on coming up, and asked Will how came he there, he answered, his life was worth no more than others, and his liberty as dear to him. I asked him if he meant to obtain it? He said he would, or lose his life. This was enough to put him in full confidence.

Such were the "bandits," as the slavocrats called them, that Nat Turner led.

In the evening of that Sunday this group of six slaves started on their crusade against slavery by killing Turner's master, Joseph Travis, together with his family. Within twenty-four hours some seventy Negroes, several mounted, had covered an area of twenty miles and had killed every human being (with an important exception), about sixty in all, that they came upon. The exception was a family of non-slaveholding poor whites who, as the Governor of Virginia sarcastically but truthfully declared, were hardly any better off than the rebels.

When within three miles of the Southampton county seat, Jerusalem (now called Courtland), there was, against Turner's advice, a fatal delay, and the Negroes—whose guns, according to the Richmond *Compiler* of August 29, were not "fit for use"—were overwhelmed by volunteer and state troops. Soon hundreds of soldiers, including cavalry and artillery units of the United States Army, swarmed over the county and, together with the inhabitants, slaughtered over one hundred slaves. Some, in the agony of death, "declared," to quote an eyewitness, "that they was going happy fore that God had a hand in what they had been doing." The killings and torturings ended when the commanding officer, General Eppes, threatened martial law.

Thirteen slaves and three free Negroes were immediately (and legally) hanged. According to Governor Floyd, "all died bravely indicating no reluctance to lose their lives in such a cause." Turner, himself, though he never left the county, was not captured until October 30. By November 5, after pleading not guilty, for, as he said, he did not feel *guilty*, he was sentenced to "be hung by the neck until you are dead! dead! dead!" on the eleventh of November. And on that day Nat Turner went calmly to his death.

The South was panic-stricken. Disaffected or rebellious slaves were, in the winter of 1831, arrested, tortured or executed in other counties of Virginia, in Delaware, Maryland, North Carolina (where at least three slave-holders died from fear!), Tennessee, Kentucky, South Carolina, Georgia, Alabama, Mississippi and Louisiana. The terror in the latter state was increased when it was discovered, according to Major-General Alexander Macomb, commanding officer of the United States Army, writing October 12, 1831, that "the coloured people in the (West Indian) Islands, had a correspondence with the Blacks of Louisiana, tending to further their insurrectionary dispositions."

There is evidence, too, that the unrest extended to poor whites as well as Negroes, at least in Virginia and North Carolina. A letter to Governor Stokes of North Carolina, from Union county, dated September 12, 1831, declared that the slave rebels there were "assisted by some rascally whites." A militia colonel of Hyde county told the same Governor on September 25 that non-slaveholding whites were refusing to join in slave-suppression activity for they said "they have no slaves of their own and ought not to be interrupted about the slaves of others." Finally, a Baltimore newspaper of October 15, 1831, stated that so far as North Carolina was concerned the "extensive and organized plan to bring about desolation and massacre...was not altogether confined to slaves."

The Governor of Virginia, in his legislative message of December 6, 1831, darkly hinted that the unrest was "not confined to the slaves." Indeed, there exists a letter from a white man, Williamson Mann, to a slave, Ben Lee, dated Chesterfield county, August 29, 1831, which confirms this. The letter makes it clear that several whites, among whom a Methodist by the name of Edmonds is especially mentioned, were plotting to aid the slaves. Mr. Mann hoped the anti-slavery efforts might succeed so that "we poor whites can get work as well as slaves."

1835-1840

The slaveholders of Madison and Hinds counties, Mississippi (where the Negro population had recently increased at a tremendous rate), became uneasy in June, 1835, due to rumors of an impending uprising. In that month a lady of the former county reported to her neighbors that she had overheard one of her slaves say, "she wished to God it was all over and done with; that she was tired of waiting on the *white folks,* and wanted to be her own mistress the balance of her days, and clean up her own house."

A favorite slave was sent among the others as a spy and soon accused one Negro. This slave, "after receiving a most severe chastisement" confessed that a plot for a revolt had been formed and implicated the slaves of a Mr. Ruel Blake, as well as that man himself. One of Mr. Blake's slaves was severely whipped, "but refused to confess anything—alleging all the time, that if they wanted to know what his master had told him, they might whip on until they killed him, that he promised that he would never divulge it."

Other slaves were tortured and it was finally discovered that there was a general plot of the slaves in the neighborhood and that a number of white men were implicated. During July about fifteen slaves and six white men were hanged. Among the white men were at least two, Joshua Cotton and William Saunders, who were notorious criminals and were interested in rebellion only for plunder's sake. It appears, however, that at least two of the white men, A. L. Donovan and R. Blake, actually hated slavery.

In October, 1835, an extensive conspiracy, said to have been instigated by white lumbermen, was unearthed and crushed in Monroe county, Georgia. This same month a plot involving at least one hundred slaves was discovered in Texas, which at the moment was rebelling against Mexico. The (slave) rebels were arrested, "many whipped nearly to death, some hung, etc." The slaves had planned to divide the land once they had conquered their masters. In December, 1835, a confidential slave betrayed a plot in East Feliciana, Louisiana. At least two whites were found to be implicated and were hanged. What happened to the slaves does not appear.

It is certain that great excitement prevailed in Tennessee and Georgia in 1836 due to reports of conspiracies and uprisings, but further details are lacking.

A conspiracy for rebellion among the slaves of Rapides parish, Louisiana, which a slaveholder described as "perfectly-planned," was betrayed in October, 1837. About forty slave leaders were arrested and at least nine of these, together with three free Negroes were hanged. After two companies of United States troops entered the zone of trouble the Negroes were "completely subdued." The betrayer of this plot was freed in 1838 and given five hundred dollars by the state to aid him in settling in some distant community.

The depression year of 1840 was very troublesome. Widespread slave disaffection was reported from Washington, D. C., from Southampton county, Virginia, from "some part of North Carolina," from Alabama and, especially, from Louisiana. The unrest in Louisiana centered in Iberville, Lafayette, St. Landry, Rapides and Avoyelles parishes. Many hundreds of slaves and several white men were arrested and scores of Negroes were legally and extra-legally killed. The massacre seems to have been most terrible in Rapides parish and it was only after a regiment of soldiers arrived "that the indiscriminate slaughter was stayed."

THE PRE-CIVIL WAR DECADE

The question of slavery agitated the nation during the decade prior to the Civil War as never before. This was the period of *Uncle Tom's Cabin* and the *Impending Crisis*, of the attack on Senator Sumner and the Dred Scott Decision, of the Kansas-Nebraska debates and the Kansas War, of the exciting elections of 1856 and 1860, and of a hundred other events forcing the slavery issue into the limelight. This reached the minds of the slaves. Moreover, an especially acute economic depression in the middle of the period, 1854-56, reached their stomachs. These, undoubtedly, are the two main reasons for the very great concerted slave unrest of the decade. Here only the most important plots and uprisings may be described.

A free Negro, George Wright, of New Orleans, was asked by a slave, Albert, in June, 1853, to join in a revolt. He declared his interest and was brought to a white man, a teacher by the name of Dyson, who had come to Louisiana in 1840 from Jamaica. Dyson trusted Wright, declared that one hundred whites had agreed to aid the Negroes in their bid for freedom, and urged Wright to join. Wright did—verbally.

He almost immediately betrayed the plot and led the police to Albert. The slaves at the time of arrest, June 13, carried a knife, a sword, a revolver, one bag of bullets, one pound of powder, two boxes of percussion caps and eighty-six dollars. The patrol was ordered out, the city guard strengthened, and twenty slaves and Dyson were instantly arrested.

Albert stated that twenty-five hundred slaves were involved. He named none. In prison he declared that "all his friends had gone down the coast and were fighting like soldiers. If he had shed blood in the cause he would not have minded the arrest." It was indeed reported by the local press that "a large number of negroes have fled from their masters and are now missing," but no actual fighting was mentioned. Excitement was great along the coast, however, and the arrest of a white man, a cattle driver, occurred at Bonnet Clare. A fisherman, Michael McGill, testified that he had taken Dyson and two slaves carrying what he thought were arms to a swamp from which several Negroes emerged. The Negroes were given the arms and disappeared.

The local papers tended to minimize the trouble, but did declare that New Orleans contained "numerous and fanatical" whites, "cutthroats in the name of liberty—murderers in the guise of philanthropy." They commended the swift action of the police and called for further precautions and restrictions. The last piece of information concerning this is an item telling of an attack by Albert upon the jailer in which he caused "the blood to flow." The disposition of the rebels is not reported.

The year 1856 was one of extraordinary slave unrest. In the summer a large group of maroon Negroes in Bladen and Robeson counties, North Carolina, became very daring and dangerous, successfully fighting off attacks by armed slaveholders. In September a conspiracy involving over two hundred slaves, together with a white man named William Mehrmann and many of "the lower class of the Mexican population," was discovered in Colorado county, Texas. The whites were forced to leave, and each of the two hundred slaves arrested was severely whipped, two dying under the lash. Three were hanged.

In October a plot involving some three hundred slaves and a few white men was reported from Ouchita and Union counties, Arkansas, and across the border in the parishes of Union and Claiborne in Louisiana. Early in November "an extensive scheme of negro insurrection" was discovered in Lavaca, DeWitt and Victoria counties, Texas. A letter from Victoria, of November 7, declared that the "negroes had killed off all the dogs in the neighborhood, and were preparing for a general attack" when betrayal came. Whites were again implicated, one being "severely horsewhipped" and the others banished. What became of the slaves is not reported. A week later an extensive conspiracy for rebellion was disclosed in St. Mary parish, Louisiana. Many slaves together with three whites and a free Negro were arrested. The slaves were lashed, and at least one of the whites together with the free Negro were hanged.

During this same month of November plots were uncovered, always with a few whites implicated, in Fayette, Obion and Montgomery counties, Tennessee, in Fulton, Kentucky, and in New Madrid and Scott counties, Missouri. Again in December conspiracies were reported, occasionally outbreaks occurred, and slaves and whites were arrested, banished, tortured, executed in virtually every slave state.

It is clear that news of this mass discontent was censored. Thus a Georgia paper, the Milledgeville *Federal Union,* admitted it had "refrained from giving our readers any of the accounts of contemplated insurrections." Similarly the New Orleans *Daily Picayune* stated it had "refrained from publishing a great deal which we receive by the mails, going to show that there is a spirit of turbulence abroad in various quarters." Later it confessed that the trouble in Kentucky, Arkansas, Tennessee, Mississippi, Louisiana and Texas amounted "very nearly to positive insurrection." Finally, the Washington correspondent of the New York *Weekly Tribune* stated on December 20 that the "insurrectionary movement in Tennessee obtained more headway than is known to the public—important facts being suppressed in order to check the spread of the contagion and prevent the true condition of affairs from being understood elsewhere." Next week the same correspondent declared that he had "reliable information" of serious trouble in New Orleans leading to the hanging of twenty slaves, "but the newspapers carefully refrain from any mention of the facts."

To the areas already mentioned as disturbed by slave disaffection may be added Maryland, Alabama, the Carolinas, Georgia and Florida. Features of the plots are worth particular notice. Arms were discovered among the slaves in, at least, Tennessee, Kentucky and Texas. Preparations for blowing up bridges were uncovered. Attacks upon iron mills in Kentucky were started but defeated. At least three slaveholders were killed in the same state. The date for the execution of four slaves in Dover, Tennessee, was pushed ahead for fear of an attempt at rescue, and a body of one hundred and fifty men was required to break up the same number of slaves marching to Dover for that very purpose.

A letter, passed along by whites as well as slaves, found December 24, 1856, on a slave employed by the Richmond and York railroad in Virginia, is interesting from the standpoint of white cooperation. It indicates, too, a desire for something more than bare bodily freedom. It reads:

My dear friend: You must certainly remember what I have told you—you must come up to the contract—as we have carried things thus far. Meet at the place where we said, and dont make any disturbance until we meet and d'ont let any white man know any-thing about it, unless he is trust-worthy. The articles are all right and the country is ours certain. Bring all your friends; tell them, that if they want freedom, to come. D'ont let it leak out; if you should get in any difficulty send me word immediately to afford protection. Meet at the crossing and prepare for Sunday night for the neighbourhood—

P.S. Dont let anybody see this—

Freedom—Freeland
Your old friend
W.B.

Another interesting feature of the plots of November and December, 1856, is the evidence of the effect of the bitter Presidential contest of that year between the Republican, Frémont, and the Democrat, Buchanan. The slaves were certain that the Republican Party stood for their liberation, and some felt that Colonel Frémont would aid them, forcibly, in their efforts for freedom. "Certain slaves are so greatly imbued with this fable that I have seen them smile when they were being whipped, and have heard them say that, 'Frémont and his men hear the blows they receive.'" One unnamed martyr, a slave iron worker in Tennessee, "said that he knew all about the plot, but would die before he would tell. He therefore received 750 lashes, from which he died."

The story of John Brown's raid has so often been told that it need not be repeated in any detail. Suffice it to say that on the night of October 16, 1859, old John Brown led twelve other white men and five Negroes (four of whom, Copeland, Leary, Anderson, Green, were escaped slaves; one, Newby, a free Negro) in an attack upon the armory in Harper's Ferry, Virginia (now West Virginia). The armory was taken, but Brown and his comrades were trapped and besieged. On October 18 a force of United States marines, led by Colonel Robert E. Lee, overpowered the rebels, seriously wounding Brown himself. The seven survivors of the battle were tried, convicted and hanged, Brown going to his death on December 2, 1859.

John Brown had in mind the establishment of centers of armed Negroes in the mountains of Virginia to which the slaves might flee and from which liberating forays might be conducted. The raid itself would not have been possible without the encouragement and financial aid offered by white and Negro abolitionists like Smith, Parker, Higginson, Sanborn, and Gloucester, Douglass, Still, Garnet.

To draw the lesson from the raid's failure that the slaves were docile, as so many writers have done, is absurd. And it would be absurd even if we did not have the record of the bitter struggle of the Negro people against enslavement. This is so for two main reasons: first, Brown's attack was made in the northwestern part of Virginia where slavery was of a domestic, household nature and where Negroes were relatively few; secondly, Brown gave the slaves absolutely no foreknowledge of his attempt. (Frederick Douglass, the great Negro leader, warned Brown that this would be fatal to his purpose.) Thus the slaves had no way of judging Brown's chances or even his sincerity, and in that connection it is important to bear in mind that slave stealing was a common crime in the old South.

Panic seized the slavocracy. Rumors of plots and revolts flew thick and fast, many undoubtedly false or exaggerated both by terror and by anti-"Black Republican" politicians. Bearing this in mind, however, there yet remains good evidence of real and widespread slave disaffection following Brown's attempt.

Serious trouble, taking the form of incendiarism, disturbed the neighborhood of Berryville, Virginia, in November, 1859. In December, Negroes in Bolivar, Missouri, revolted and attacked their enslavers with sticks and stones. A few whites were injured and at least one slave was killed. Later, according to a local paper:

A mounted company was ranging the woods in search of negroes. The owner of some rebellious slaves was badly wounded, and only saved himself by flight. Several blacks have been severely punished. The greatest excitement prevailed, and every man was armed and prepared for a more serious attack.

Still later advices declared that "the excitement had somewhat subsided." What this "subsidence" meant in human suffering is unknown.

The years from 1860 through 1864 were filled with slave revolts and conspiracies. These have been described in detail in the writer's work, "The Negro in the Civil War" (written in 1938). Here it need merely be stated that, in these years, poor whites were almost invariably implicated as allies of the Negro slaves. Furthermore, at times, the plots very definitely had aims other than the end of slavery, such as distribution of the land, the work animals and the tools to the common people of the South. And the entire South was involved, from Maryland to Florida, from Kentucky to Texas.

III. EFFECTS OF THE REVOLTS AND CONSPIRACIES

There are few phases of ante-bellum Southern life and history that were not in some way influenced by the fear of, or the actual occurrence of, slave uprisings. In some cases the influences were plainly of a minor, if not of a merely formal nature. Such was surely the case when

Southerners appealed in 1803 for the annexation of Louisiana in order to take it out of the hands of a possibly hostile and apparently revolutionary France, which might use that possession as a means of arousing slave rebellion in the United States. Similar arguments were used to justify the annexation of Texas and Florida.

Another argument, however, used in the Louisiana annexation case and in every subsequent territorial advance of the slavocracy, to the effect that the South needed new lands in order to lessen the danger of slave rebellion by checking the concentration of Negroes within a limited area, seems to have been a fairly important consideration in the minds of Southern leaders.

The possibility of slave rebellion, the necessity of guarding one-third of the population, and the inadvisability of arming that proportion of the population, created serious military difficulties for the United States and later, and particularly for the Confederate States. When, for example, during the Revolution, South Carolina learned that the Continental Congress was seriously contemplating the wholesale arming of the slaves to fight the British (with future manumission understood), she threatened to withdraw from the contest with England and return to a colonial status. And, in other ways, throughout the Revolutionary War and the War of 1812, the United States was made keenly aware of military weakness due to the fear of servile disaffection. Similarly, as has been shown in the work previously referred to, this fear, and its not infrequent justification in actual outbreak, was a major military disadvantage to the Confederate States.

During years of national peace the military might of the United States government was concentrated in the Southern region, undoubtedly because of fear of rebellion. The use of this might for purposes of slave suppression occurred in Virginia in 1800, in Louisiana in 1811, in

Florida in 1816 and 1820, in South Carolina in 1822, in Virginia in 1831, in Louisiana in 1837, in Florida again during the Second Seminole War from 1836-43, and in Virginia in 1859.

The South itself was, so far as about one-third of its population was concerned, a huge fortress in which prisoners were held, at hard labor, for life. Like any other fortress it was exceedingly well guarded. Militarism was a dominant characteristic of the region and was noticed by virtually every visitor. As an English traveler, Francis Baily remarked in 1796, every white man was a soldier. The carrying of some type of weapon was a universal characteristic of Southern white men. Well-trained militia companies and volunteer military units were numerous, patrols were everywhere, armed overseers were on all plantations, guards and standing armies (like the seventy soldiers maintained by Richmond after Gabriel's conspiracy of 1800) abounded in the cities. Slavery was a chronic state of warfare, and all men who were not Negroes were, *by law*, part of the standing army of oppressors.

The violence and militarism, the chronic state of war, were most important factors in arousing opposition to the slave system amongst non-slaveholders. This is especially true of the Quaker element in the South; mass migrations of those devout people occurred particularly after periods of serious slave unrest. This was especially true in the years from about 1795-1805 and again from 1828-32, when thousands of Quakers from Virginia to Georgia removed from the South into Pennsylvania and the Northwest. It is also to be noted that there is evidence of migrations of other non-slaveholders, during serious slave unrest, from the very simple motive of fear. Why remain in an area subject to intermittent upheavals?

It has been mentioned that all white male citizens of the South were subject to patrol duty. The brunt, however, of this arduous duty fell upon the poor whites, not only because they were most numerous, but also because the wealthier whites easily paid the fine of from one dollar to five dollars for failure to perform patrol duty. This was of course impossible to the poor whites, and this class distinction aroused bitterness, especially since patroling was often dangerous and rarely pleasant. Another grievance of non-slaveholding whites arose from the fact that they were taxed (in common, of course, with slaveholders; though in some states, as North Carolina, the tax system favored the slaveholders) to support the slave suppression apparatus. Moreover, masters whose slaves were executed by the state were reimbursed the approximate value of the slave and this, again, added to the non-slaveholders' tax bills.

Fear of slave disaffection was a factor in the widespread Southern opposition to urbanization and industrialization. Undoubtedly of greatest importance in keeping the pre-war South rural and agrarian was the fact that the institution of slavery froze billions of dollars of capital into human beings. Nevertheless the fear that proletarianized Negroes, congregated in common centers, would be more difficult to hold in enslavement was widespread, and did much to discourage large-scale manufacturing.

It has been shown that the prevalence of revolutionary sentiments and slogans invariably reached the consciousness of America's slaves and affected their behavior. The slavocrats were keenly aware of this. The irreconcilability of a progressive political philosophy with the persistence of plantation slavery was well understood in the South. The fear that the former would lead to the destruction of the latter did much to hasten the South in its repudiation of Jeffersonian equalitarian doctrines. A Virginia aristocrat back in 1794 pointed out that the democrats favored the common, poor people and asked, "Who so poor as our

63

slaves, who therefore so fit to participate in the spoils of the rich and to direct the affairs of the nation?" This is certainly a factor explaining the dominance of anti-Jeffersonianism in cities like Richmond and Charleston, and in the early substitution by the South of a superior "race" and property-rule philosophy for the Jeffersonian ideas of equality and democracy.

Slave rebellion at times frightened the ruling class into granting some concessions, as the establishing of legal minima of provisions for the Negroes. This occurred in South Carolina in 1740 and in Louisiana in 1795. More often it led the Bourbons to pass laws restricting or forbidding the foreign or the domestic slave trade. Other factors than fear were often behind such laws, as the desire to boost the price of the slaves already in the state, or, particularly from 1770 to about 1790, the widespread influence of the Jeffersonian concepts of individual freedom and economic independence, leading to opposition to slavery and, especially, to the slave trade. Yet the aim of cutting down slave outbreaks appears to have been the dominant motive. The period of the most numerous and most drastic anti-slave trade laws coincides with that period of most serious slave unrest, 1791-1802. These enactments (passed by the Federal government in 1794, 1800; by South Carolina in 1792, 1794, 1796, 1800, 1801; North Carolina, 1794; New Jersey, 1798; Maryland, 1796; Louisiana, 1796), indeed, had they not usually been quickly repealed and always laxly enforced, might well have caused the death of slavery.

As a matter of fact, other acts or bills having this, the end of slavery in view, were passed or nearly passed, throughout the nation during the 1790's. During that decade of depression and unprecedented slave unrest (in the West Indies as well as here), the slaveholders of the border areas came the closest they were ever to come to the peaceful abolition of slavery. Manumission was made easier in Maryland (1796), in New Jersey (1798), Kentucky (1798, 1800), Tennessee (1801). Serious, though futile, attempts were made in Maryland and Kentucky in 1799 to enact laws for gradual emancipation. The Territory of Mississippi had the same experience in 1798, and in 1802 a bill to forbid the importation into that Territory, for any purpose, of all male Negro slaves, passed the House but was defeated in the Council by two votes. These years, too, mark the enactment of emancipation laws in the Northern states. To the conventional reasons for this—relatively small number of slaves and unprofitableness of slavery in the North—is to be added the fear aroused by the examples of mass slave rebellion in the South, as well as a taste of this at home in the widespread arson activities of slaves in New York, Philadelphia, Newark, and Elizabeth, New Jersey, in 1796.

But the great plantation oligarchs of eastern Virginia and North Carolina, of South Carolina, Georgia and Louisiana, never seriously considered the elimination of slavery. With the return of prosperity in about 1802 (earlier in Louisiana) and the tremendous spurt in cotton and sugar production (together with, in 1803, the annexation of Louisiana), slavery became fastened upon the South.

Slavery was, then, not to be abolished but rather encouraged and fostered. Unrest was to be expected but a policy of blood and iron would, nevertheless, maintain the institution. To quote a Virginia slaveholder of 1800: "In a word, if we will keep a ferocious monster in our country, we must keep him in chains."

The forging and refurbishing of these chains always followed slave rebellions. Every conceivable legal device was made use of to keep the Negroes in bondage. The whole system of oppression has been mentioned—military might, chauvinism, enforced ignorance, and the denial of freedom of speech, of press, of petition and of religion so far as the slave question was concerned.

Fear of slave rebellion was also the motivating force behind the movement for the colonization of free or freed Negroes in some area (Africa was favored) outside the United States. One of the earliest proposals of that kind was made in 1772 by a citizen of New Jersey after the discovery of a slave plot there. From then on every conspiracy or uprising renewed propaganda for the idea. There was considerable agitation for it after the Gabriel conspiracy in Virginia in 1800, but the Colonization Society was not formed until December, 1816, a year, it will be remembered, of considerable unrest.

Its essential purpose was well stated by John Randolph, speaking at its first meeting in Washington. He declared that the aim of the movement was "to secure the property of every master to, in, and over his slaves." It was to do this by removing the free Negroes who were "one of the greatest sources of the insecurity" of slaveholding since, by their very existence, "they excited discontent" among the slaves.

Periods of increased slave discontent were periods of increased activity for this Society (until about 1835 when its impotence was clear to all). Yet, although most "respectable" channels of propaganda were friendly to it, and although wealthy individuals and Southern states liberally provided it with funds, the movement was a total failure. In its first (and most active) sixteen years of existence the Society managed to colonize only 2,203 Negroes. The essential reason for its utter failure was, from its beginning, the bitter and well-nigh unanimous opposition of the Negro people to any movement seeking to remove them from their native land and, by doing that, more securely enslave their brethren.

66

Colonization depended only upon persuasion. But, especially following serious manifestations of unrest, legal and extra-legal forces were brought to bear to make life in the South miserable for the free Negroes, and so force them to leave. All sorts of laws depriving these Negroes of civil and economic rights were passed with this in mind. Threats of violence were also not infrequent and, especially after the Turner revolt, caused the removal of many free Negroes. Just before the Civil War the desperate slavocracy was moving toward the enslavement of all free Negroes. Arkansas, in 1859, ordered all free Negroes to leave under pain of being sold into slavery, and both Florida and Georgia enacted laws requiring the enslavement of all "idle" or "vagrant" free Negroes. This created a mass exodus of free Negroes (what would today be called a "refugee problem"). Within three years many of these exiles were marching back into Arkansas and Florida and Georgia with guns on their shoulders and the song, "John Brown's Body," on their lips.

Walt Whitman once declared that "where liberty draws not the blood out of slavery, there slavery draws the blood out of liberty." The slavocrats knew this and applied it first in their own bailiwick. For in the slave South freedom was but a shadow. By the 1820's the Bourbons had avowedly turned against the Declaration of Independence and denounced it as a ridiculous, and dangerous, concoction of glittering generalities. Of course one-third of the population of the South was beyond its pale, but, and here's the point, to keep them beyond the pale it was necessary to vitiate everyone's freedom, it was necessary to "draw the blood out of liberty." First came the free Negroes and then the non-slaveholding whites. Their religion, their speech, their writings, their teachings had to conform to the slave system. If not they were forced to leave, lashed, tarred and feathered, or killed.

And you in the North are to say nothing. Slavery is our affair; we demand "non-intervention." But this "non-intervention" (the thoroughly modern term was then used) is only to work one way. You are not to interfere in our affairs, but we may in yours; we demand that you curb your "fanatics," stop denouncing slavery, stop sheltering fugitives, continue supporting an army to be used to overawe and suppress our slaves. We refuse to accept your petitions against slavery or, indeed, any petition having the faintest connection with slavery (so that the Congress of the United States actually tabled the Declaration of Independence when offered as a petition!), and we refuse to transmit your anti-slavery writings through the mail. Your Negro seamen are dangerous to us and we refuse to admit them into our ports. In a word, we may and will do what we think is necessary for the security of our slave property. If that restricts your activities or liberties, it is just too bad.

This inevitable broadening of the anti-slavery struggle into a battle for the maintenance of the democratic rights of the white people, as well as the obtaining of those rights for the Negro people, was probably the most important strengthening force of the entire Abolitionist movement. And one of the great causes of this nationalization of the anti-slavery crusade was the fear of slave rebellions and the measures taken to prevent or subdue their occurrence.

At least one other important effect of the slave rebellions is apparent. This is the added drive that they directly gave to the Abolitionist movement. The slavocrats were forever prating about the docility of their slaves, their lack of desire for freedom, and the delightful conditions of slavery. But here, time and again, came news of slaves conspiring and dying in an effort to leave the blessed state of Southern "patriarchal" slavery. Peculiar activity for docile men and women! Peculiar activity for human beings who did not want freedom!

Thus Abolitionists would declare, following a revolt: "Insurrections are the natural and consequent productions of slavery—experience has proved this in all ages and in all nations where slavery has existed. Slavery *ought* to be, must be, and shall be abolished in these United States." Or, in the inimitable words of William Lloyd Garrison, addressed to slaveholders after Nat Turner's outbreak:

Ye patriotic hypocrites!...ye Christian declaimers for liberty! ye valiant sticklers for equal rights among yourselves! ye haters of aristocracy! ye assailants of monarchy! ye republican nullifiers! ye treasonable disunionists! be dumb! Cast no reproach upon the conduct of the slaves, but let your lips and cheeks wear the blisters of condemnation!

There is, too, clear evidence of the inspiration which immortal John Brown drew from Nat Turner (one of the old man's heroes) and from the widespread slave discontent manifested in 1856. Both added to his hatred of slavery and his respect for the Negro people, and were influential in moving him to strike his noble and world-shaking blow against human bondage.

American slavery was a barbarous tyranny. It impoverished the land and the common people, Negro and white, of the South, tore away their freedom and attempted to destroy the liberty of all American citizens.

Its history, however, is not merely one of impoverishment, deprivation, and oppression. For imbedded in the record of American slavery is the inspiring story of the persistent and courageous efforts of the Negroes (aided, not infrequently, by the poor whites) to regain their heritage of liberty and equality, to regain their right to the elemental demands of human beings.

The effects of this struggle were national and world-shaking in its day. An awareness of its history should give the modern Negro added confidence and courage in his heroic present-day battle for complete and perfect equality with all other American citizens. And it should make those other Americans eager and proud to grasp the hand of the Negro and march forward with him against their common oppressors—against these industrial and financial overlords and the plantation oligarchs who today stand in the way of liberty, equality and prosperity.

That unity between the white and Negro masses was necessary to overthrow nineteenth-century slavery. That same unity is necessary now to defeat twentieth-century slavery—to defeat fascism.

THE NEGRO IN THE AMERICAN
REVOLUTION

I. INTRODUCTION

The desire for freedom is the central theme, the motivating force, in the history of the American Negro people. This has always determined their actions, policies and efforts, and has, indeed, permeated their religions, inspired their real and legendary heroes, and filled their incomparably beautiful hymns and spirituals.

Centuries of unspeakable suffering and dire privation have developed among the American Negro people an unlimited sympathy for all progressive movements and an impelling, urgent yearning for their own liberation. These things are true now and they were true at the birthing-time of our nation.

The chain-breaking features of the first American Revolution—its denunciation of aristocracy, its separation of Church and State, its espousal of a nation's right to self-determination, its overthrow of feudal hangovers, its promise of liberty and equality, its proud avowal of man's right and ability to direct his own destiny and guide his own pursuit of happiness here and now, not hereafter and in some nebulous beyond—won the whole-hearted support of the Negro people. Those among them who were free rushed forward to offer their services and one of them, an escaped slave named Crispus Attucks (in whom, fittingly enough, flowed white and Indian blood as well as Negro), was the first to die challenging the rule of Britain, falling dead in Boston, his chest pierced by two bullets, five years before the Battle of Lexington.

But the Negro people, particularly the vast majority who were slaves, were to meet disappointment. They were to learn that many of the Revolutionists who cried "liberty, equality," meant to add, "for whites only," and that some did not even mean that. Gouverneur Morris, for example, wrote in 1774 that "The mob begins to think and reason. Poor reptiles! it is with them a vernal morning; they are struggling to cast off their winter's slough, they bask in the sunshine and ere noon they will bite." And Morris was not going to be bitten if he could avoid it. Still others, who were also part of this First American Revolution, bought and sold and branded and beat and owned human beings and meant to go right on owning men and women (while talking about freedom and equality).

Thus it came about that the Negro people played what at first glance appears to have been a dual role here from 1775 to 1783. Where and when possible, that is, where and when they were permitted to do so, and given freedom for doing so, Negroes served the forces which were in rebellion against British tyranny, but where and when this was not possible they fled to the British armies, or to Florida, or to Canada, and some actually fought in the King's army. And where this, too, was not possible, some fled into neighboring swamps, forests, and mountains resisting whomsoever sought to re-enslave them; still others, finding escape impossible, conspired or rebelled for freedom.

But these varied and superficially contradictory activities have one common origin, one set purpose—the achievement of liberty. This was and is the American Negro's guiding star. With this in mind let us examine the activities of these 500,000 inhabitants of a nation in rebellion, a nation whose total population, Negro and white, was only two and a half millions.

II. THE GROWTH IN ANTI-SLAVERY FEELING

The struggle of the American colonies for political and economic freedom from Great Britain gave a considerable impetus to the anti-slavery movement. This was anxiously watched and, where possible, aided by the Negro people themselves. In order fully to appreciate the role of the Negro in the American Revolution it is necessary to trace the story of this development and to observe that while some definite advancement was made yet no general clear-cut victory was achieved.

In the early literature, setting the stage for the revolutionary upsurge, notice is taken of the inconsistency in struggling for political and economic freedom while depriving hundreds of thousands of their personal freedom. This may, for example, be found in the writings of James Otis, the early leading theoretician of the Revolution, who, in his famous pamphlet called *Rights of the British Colonies* published in Boston in 1764, denounced slavery, affirmed the Negro's inalienable right to freedom and, at least by implication, upheld his right instantly to rebel against his enslavers.

Some of the later literature became even more bold, as when the Reverend Isaac Skillman in his *Oration upon the Beauties of Liberty* (published in Boston in 1772, and in its fourth printing by 1773) demanded the immediate abolition of slavery. In this work the reverend gentleman went as far as abolition literature was ever to go in asserting the slave's right to rebel, for, said he, this act would conform "to the laws of nature."

These same years witnessed the height of Anthony Benezet's anti-slavery work, as well as that of Benjamin Franklin and Benjamin Rush, each of whom widely spread his views. It is also an interesting sign of the spirit of the times to note that the addresses delivered at the commencement exercises of Harvard University at Cambridge, Massachusetts, in July, 1773, were concerned with "the legality of enslaving the Africans." Similar sentiments were expressed by Abigail Adams in telling her husband, John, in September, 1774, upon the discovery of a slave conspiracy in Boston, that "it always appeared a most iniquitous scheme to me to fight ourselves for what we are daily robbing and plundering from those who have as good a right to freedom as we have."

And it is to be remembered that the first article Thomas Paine, the international tribune of the people, ever wrote for publication was entitled "African Slavery in America" and appeared in a Pennsylvania paper of March 8, 1775. In this work Paine denounced slavery, demanded that it be abolished and that the Negroes be given land and the opportunity of earning a livelihood as well as personal liberty.

There are, too, besides these instances of individual protest (and the above is meant only as a sampling of that type of anti-slavery activity) many evidences of organized opposition to the institution of slavery during the Revolutionary period. Of very considerable importance in this activity, even during this early period, was the work of the Negro people themselves. We have, for example, evidence in John Adams' diary note of November 5, 1766, that Massachusetts slaves attempted, by bringing an action of trespass in the local courts against their masters, to challenge the entire legal concept of slavery. Adams, in reporting his own presence at one such unsuccessful effort, remarked that he had "heard there have been many." But this type of action proved futile.

The Negro people then turned to the application of mass pressure by the presentation of petitions to the legislatures appealing for liberation. There is record of at least eight such attempts, the first of which, appealing for the possibility of earning money with which to purchase freedom, was presented to the Massachusetts General Court in April, 1773. Two months later other slaves petitioned Governor Gage and the same General Court to grant them their freedom, together with land, for, said the Negroes, "they have in common with other men a natural right to be free." Still another "Petition of a Grate Number of Blackes" reached these same individuals in May, 1774, again asking for freedom as a natural right and denouncing slavery as sinful and evil. The next month, and the next year, still other petitions, of similar tenor, were presented.

In the spring of 1775 the Negroes of Bristol and Worcester in Massachusetts petitioned the Committee of Correspondence of the latter county to aid them in obtaining freedom. This resulted in a convention held in Worcester on June 14 at which it was resolved by the white inhabitants present "That we abhor the enslaving of any of the human race, and particularly of the Negroes in this country, and that whenever there shall be a door opened, or opportunity present for anything to be done towards the emancipation of the Negroes, we will use our influence and endeavor that such a thing may be brought about." Again, in January, 1777, many slaves of Massachusetts presented to the Council and House of Representatives of that State a prayer for freedom remarking that "they Cannot but express their Astonishment that It has Never Bin Considered that Every Principle from which America has Acted in the Cours of their unhappy Deficulties with

77

Great Britain Pleads Stronger than A thousand arguments in favours of your petitioners."

Finally, so far as the available records show, there was the interesting petition for liberty presented by twenty Negroes of Portsmouth in November, 1779, to the New Hampshire legislature. This declared, in the precise reasoning of the Revolutionary movement itself, "That the God of Nature gave them life and freedom, upon the terms of most perfect equality with other men; That freedom is an inherent right of the human species, not to be surrendered, but by consent, for the sake of social life."

Protests against slavery having an organized and mass origin also arose from the midst of the white people. Thus the religious Society of Friends, or Quakers, made considerable advances during the years of the Revolution towards wiping slavetrading and slaveholding out of their group and by about 1785 this had generally been accomplished.

Governmental groups also took some steps in that direction. In 1770 several petitions urging the end of slavery were received by the Connecticut legislature, which the next year forbade the slave trade. The New Jersey Assembly also received, in 1773, anti-slavery petitions from groups of citizens in six counties. Rhode Island declared, in 1774, that any Negro slave thereafter brought into the region was to be free, and the preamble to this law stated that this action was taken because "the inhabitants of America are generally engaged in the preservation of their own rights and liberties, among which that of personal freedom must be considered as the greatest, and as those who are desirous of enjoying all the advantages of liberty themselves should be willing to extend personal liberty to others." It is, however, to be observed that the law did not free the slaves (of which there were some 3,500) then in Rhode Island, though later legislation permitting them to join the army did, as we shall see later, have the effect of liberating several hundreds of Negroes in that state.

Other legal acts or declarations of an anti-slavery outlook were common. The Braintree, Massachusetts, town meeting, for example, early in 1774 adopted a resolution promising to abstain from the slave trade and to boycott all who engaged in that business. Within a year of this action other localities, such as Providence, Rhode Island; Chester County, Pennsylvania; Delaware and Georgia, either considered or passed similar measures. The New York City delegation to the Provincial Congress of the State, headed by John Jay, future first Chief Justice of the United States Supreme Court, urged, in 1777, the adoption of a gradual emancipation law. This came close to adoption and might well have been passed had not John Jay been forced to absent himself due to the death of his mother. Twenty-two years were to pass before New York enacted such a law.

The constitution adopted in Vermont in July, 1777, contained a specific clause appended to the Declaration of Rights directly forbidding the enslavement of any individual, whether "born in this country or brought from over sea." In 1780 an emancipation bill was considered by the Connecticut legislature. A law gradually abolishing slavery, and written by Thomas Paine and George Bryan, was passed in Pennsylvania on March 1, 1780.

The liberty and equality clauses in the Massachusetts constitution of 1781 and in the New Hampshire constitution of 1784 were generally considered to have ended, for all practical purposes, the institution of slavery in those states, while in the latter year, 1784, Connecticut enacted a gradual emancipation law. It is also to be noted that Virginia in May, 1782, considerably eased the requirements for the manumission of slaves, but this liberal law, under

79

which hundreds of Negroes were granted their freedom, was repealed within five years.

Similar tendencies came forward too, though rather weakly, on the national scene. Thus, part of the agreement reached in the Continental Association of 1774 called for an end to the foreign slave trade as an expression of both an anti-slavery and an anti-British feeling, the latter because the commerce in slaves was, to a considerable extent, carried on by English merchants. The Continental Congress repeated this action in April, 1776, by resolving that the importation of slaves should stop.

There was, of course, latent anti-slavery sentiment in the final Declaration of Independence, particularly in its brave assertions "that all men are created equal, that they are endowed with certain unalienable Rights, that among these are Life, Liberty, and the pursuit of Happiness." It is, moreover, interesting to note that Jefferson's original draft of this immortal manifesto of revolution contained an overt and powerful anti-slavery declaration. In his list of grievances against the British monarch, Jefferson had originally included this statement:

He has waged cruel war against human nature itself, violating its most sacred rights of life and liberty in the persons of a distant people who never offended him, captivating and carrying them into slavery in another hemisphere, or to incur miserable death in their transportation thither. This piratical warfare, the opprobrium of *infidel* powers, is the warfare of this *Christian* king of Great Britain determined to keep open a market where MEN should be bought and sold.

But this was, at the request of delegates from South Carolina and Georgia, and certain of the slave-trading New England states, deleted from the final copy. Other acts of an even more reprehensible character must be told if we are to understand the actions of a huge number of slaves in seeking freedom where they could—and particularly by flight to the armies of the British.

North Carolina, for example, passed a law in 1777 making the manumission of slaves difficult because "the evil and pernicious Practice of freeing Slaves in this State, ought at this alarming and critical Time to be guarded against by every friend and Well-wisher to his Country." South Carolina, in 1780, reached the depths of infamy, for it then passed a law granting a prime slave as part of the bounty to be given to soldiers volunteering for service in the Revolutionary army. As a matter of fact, this state, together with Georgia, made a practice of partly paying their officials' salaries by giving them slaves.

It may then be declared that the Negro people did receive some benefits from their own agitational efforts and from the increase in anti-slavery sentiment that accompanied the Revolutionary movement, but it is necessary to observe that these benefits generally came late in the period, were rarely far-reaching, and that the attitude of the Southern states, where, of course, the real evil of slavery was concentrated, was not one warranting hope or enthusiasm on the part of the Negro people. Where the Negro could serve his native land and obtain his freedom he gladly did so, but where he discovered that his native land denied him his craving for liberation he turned elsewhere—to arson, rebellion, flight—for it was liberty he wanted, not high-sounding speeches.

III. EFFORTS FOR FREEDOM

SPECIAL PRECAUTIONS OF THE SLAVOCRACY

Any unusual excitement always resulted in increased restlessness and more widespread disaffection among America's slaves. The era of the Revolution is an outstanding example of that fact. The slaveowners knew this and accordingly adopted extraordinary precautions. They knew, as two of them, Archibald Bullock and John Houston, told John Adams on November 24, 1775, that were an officer to land his army within the Southern slave area "and proclaim freedom to all the Negroes who would join his camp, twenty thousand Negroes would join it... in a fortnight." For, as these same men remarked, "The Negroes have a wonderful art of communicating intelligence among themselves; it will run several hundreds of miles in a week or fortnight."

The slave area always operated under strict military, legal, and social systems of control (see pages 3-70 in this volume) but during this period of turmoil special safeguards were instituted.

A general policy of removing the slave population from zones close to the British armies was followed. Thus, the Virginia Committee of Safety ordered on April 10, 1776, the removal of all slaves above thirteen years of age from the eastern counties of Norfolk and Princess Anne further inland and away from the British forces. The Congress of North Carolina a month later ordered that masters compel all adult male slaves south of Cape Fear River to move further inland, "into the country, remote from the Sea."

In September, 1777, the Council of Virginia after reciting the fact that "many Negroes" had fled, empowered the Governor to cause them to be moved whenever and wherever he pleased. The Assembly of Virginia, moreover, passed an act making it possible for planters of other states to ship their slaves to the interior of Virginia, and it is certain that this was taken advantage of by some in Georgia and the Carolinas.

Virginia also, in December, 1775, passed an act permitting the sale, banishment, or execution of Negroes caught attempting to flee. And this law was enforced as is demonstrated by the hanging in March, 1776, of four captured runaways, and the sale and transportation to the West Indies, in January, 1776, of about twenty-five others. The money from these sales was turned over to their masters "provided they are not unfriendly to American liberty"! Sale and banishment of Negroes caught attempting to gain their liberty by flight occurred elsewhere, as in Albany, New York, in March, 1778, when four slaves were so treated. Three others involved in the same effort received fifty lashes each.

Other special precautions were used as when Georgia, in August, 1776, confined certain Negro pilots and stationed a guard boat in Savannah "to prevent Negroes from going down to Cockspur," an island off which were stationed enemy vessels. Similar action was taken elsewhere, as in St. Mary's County, Maryland, from whence an officer reported in March, 1781, that he had posted guards "at the most convenient places to prevent the Negroes from going to the Enemy & Secured all Boats & Canoes." Another officer that same month asked Maryland's Governor for sixty more men to be kept "constantly patroling" in St. Mary's County in order to prevent the flight of slaves, "as from the late conduct of the Negroes when those ships (of the British) were in St. Marys I am

83

well satisfied the greatest part of them that are in the County would join them."

FLIGHT

Yet with all this—the lashes, deportations, hangings, forcible removals, added patrols, withdrawal of boats—tens of thousands of slaves succeeded in escaping, but too often, the evidence demonstrates, only to meet bad treatment, disease and death, and even, some evidence seems to show, sale into West Indian slavery, at the hands of the British. It is indeed likely that news of the evils generally awaiting slaves who managed to reach the English forces did more to discourage flight, in that particular direction, than all the repressions and precautions practiced by the Revolutionists.

References to and complaints about the wholesale flight of slaves may be observed as soon as the fighting began. The royal governor of Virginia, Lord Dunmore, attempted to cripple the revolution by offering, in a public proclamation of November 7, 1775, to give freedom to the slaves of all "rebels" who were able to bear arms and who reached his lines. The Virginia Committee of Safety, realizing the gravity of the situation, promptly issued a counter-proclamation. This warned the slaves not to heed Dunmore's offer, and pointed out that Great Britain herself owned slaves whom it did not offer freedom, that she had been the greatest stimulator of the slave trade and had, indeed, vetoed Virginia's efforts at suppressing that trade. Moreover, said Virginia's proclamation, Dunmore's offer extended only to the adult male slaves (who would thus have to abandon their families) of the "rebels," not of the Tories, and he probably would betray the promise anyway and ship the Negroes to the West Indies. Added to this appeal, as has been mentioneed, was Virginia's law

84

of December, 1775, providing banishment or execution as the penalties for captured fugitive slaves.

Nevertheless the passion for liberty among the Negro people was so great, the yearning for freedom burned so intensely within them, that literally thousands immediately attempted to flee. The prominent Virginian, Edmund Pendleton, told Richard Henry Lee on November 27, 1775, that "slaves flock to him [Dunmore] in abundance," and two weeks later an American lady told her London friend that: "The flame runs like wild fire through the slaves." Local Virginia county committees in November and December, 1775, like those of Northampton and Warwick also refer to the wholesale exodus of the slave population. The letters of Dunmore himself testify to this same situation and add the tragic information that most of the fugitives found disease and death instead of freedom within the British lines. As one example may be cited Dunmore's letter written June 26, 1776, from Gwin's Island Harbor, Virginia, to Lord Germaine, the British Secretary of State, which declared that many slaves had fled to him but that sickness "has carried off an incredible number of our people, especially the blacks."

Similar conditions prevailed elsewhere. The Georgia Council of Safety on July 5, 1776, complained of the general flight of the slaves of eastern Georgia. Again, the comment of an American officer, Major Thomas Price, in a letter to the Maryland Council of Safety, is illuminating. He stated on July 23, 1776, that: "A valuable Negro made his escape from us last night, he not being so well guarded as he ought to have been.... The shores are full of dead bodies, chiefly Negroes," washed ashore from the British boats. A little later, September 9, 1776, a Mr. Charles Read of Burlington, New Jersey, advertised the flight of his slave, Moses, and added this note, "As he has been endeavoring to prevail upon the Negroes in this Neighbourhood to go with him, and join the ministerial army, it is hoped every lover of his country will endeavor to apprehend so daring a villain."

These efforts to gain freedom by flight continued throughout the war years. Thus, we find the Council of the Virginia legislature referring on September 5, 1777, to the escape of "many Negroes" from "The Counties of Northampton and Accomack on the Eastern shore" and expressing fear that "many more will follow their Example." Similar references to flights recur in the Council records of Maryland during 1777 and 1778. And a Mr. Tazewell wrote in June, 1779, from Williamsburg of the flight of five hundred slaves from Norfolk County, Virginia. The march of General Prevost's British army through South Carolina in 1779 likewise resulted in the flight of thousands of slaves with, again, abominable conditions and treatment leading to the deaths of hundreds. It is also to be noted that Tories who fled from territory under the domination of the revolutionists, particularly in South Carolina and Georgia, and attempted to take their slaves with them, suffered great losses by the flight of the Negroes, many of whom met death through disease and starvation.

To the very days of the cessation of fighting this desperate exodus went on. Glimpses of the story break through, as the conviction of a slave, Jack, of Botetourt County, Virginia, in April, 1780, of attempting to lead many slaves to Cornwallis' army and of his being sentenced to hang. Up in Albany, New York, six Negroes were jailed in May, 1780, for attempting, with the aid of a white man named Joseph Bettis, to flee to Canada. Down in Virginia, that same month, according to Joseph Jones, slaveholders still complained because of "their Negroes flying from them," while in November, 1780, Lt. Col. Murfree told Governor Nash of North Carolina that "A great many (North Carolina) Negroes goes (sic) to the Enemy." Again in July, 1781, another Virginian, Richard Henry Lee, told his brother William that "Your neighbors Colo. Taliaferro & Colo. Travis lost every slave they had in the world, and Mr. Paradise has lost all his but one. This has been the general case of all those who were near the enemy."

Some idea of the extent of this flight over the whole period of the Revolution may be obtained by considering certain contemporary figures. Thus, for example, after the Treaty of Paris of 1783 ending the war, the British armies sailed away from New York City with well over three thousand escaped Negroes, for the United States commissioners, sent to discover how many fugitives were aboard the ships of the British fleet in that harbor, actually counted 2,997, while crowded ships were secretly dispatched by British officers who feared their government might have to pay for each Negro taken away. (The question of reparation for slaves who reached English forces was a sore one between Great Britain and the United States for several years, but England refused to compensate this government.) When the British fleet evacuated Savannah, Georgia, in July, 1782, it carried away some five thousand escaped slaves, and about six thousand five hundred Negroes sailed away in 1783, when the British withdrew from Charleston, South Carolina. In addition, it is to be kept in mind that all through the seven years of fighting ships filled with escaped slaves were again and again sent to Florida, the West Indies, England, and Nova Scotia by the British, in practically all cases, unfortunately, to suffer fearful oppression as peons, if not actually slaves. Many, moreover, fled to areas within the United States, and to the armies of the French ally, as well as to the British.

Contemporary estimates of total losses offer further

enlightenment. Thomas Jefferson declared that in the one year of 1778 Virginia alone saw thirty thousand slaves flee from bondage, and we know that many more escaped both before and after that year. Georgians felt that from 75 to 85 per cent of their slaves (who numbered about fifteen thousand in 1774) fled, and South Carolinians declared that of their total number of some one hundred and ten thousand slaves at the start of the Revolution, at least twenty-five thousand made good their escape. It is certainly a fact that although South Carolina imported slaves by the thousands in the years immediately after the Revolution she did not again have as many slaves as she had had in 1773 until the year 1790. If to all this one adds the slaves who escaped from North Carolina, Maryland, Delaware, and the Northern states, particularly New York and New Jersey, it appears to be conservative to say that from 1775 until 1783 some one hundred thousand slaves (*i.e.,* about one out of every five) *succeeded* in escaping from slavery, though very often meeting death or serfdom instead of liberty.

It was very fortunate for the revolutionary cause that political and economic considerations restrained the British from actively waging an anti-slavery war and thus gaining twice or three times the number of refugees she did and actively using them against the Americans. But it is to be borne in mind that the English empire was itself the enslaver of tens of thousands of Negroes in the West Indies and that many of the Tories in the Southern area were large slaveholders.

These Tory and West Indian slaveholders needed British aid in maintaining their ownership of the Negroes (the British fleet and troops stationed in the West Indies were absolutely necessary for the security of slavery there, and this was an important consideration in the minds of discontented Islanders for not joining their Continental brethren in rebellion against British imperialism—a reminder of this came to Jamaica in 1776 in the form of a serious slave revolt) and thus it was that the English offered freedom only to male adult slaves of the rebels, treated even them badly, and enlisted few as soldiers. Several hundred American Negroes did, however, secure their liberty by serving in the British armies, particularly those of Dunmore in Virginia, Prevost in Georgia, and Leslie in South Carolina.

CONSPIRACY, REBELLION

Contemporary evidence demonstrates that not a few of the slaves fled to neighboring swamps, forests, and mountains and at times waged their own guerrilla warfare against slaveholders. Thus an engagement between twenty-one maroons (on whose side fought five unidentified whites) and slaveholders was reported from eastern Georgia in September, 1776, with, it was said, two slaveholders and eleven Negroes being killed.

North Carolina passed a law in 1778 permitting the hunting, capturing, and sale of all fugitives and explained that this was needed for "many Negroes are now going at large to the Terror of the good People of this State." A letter from George Washington to General John Stark of October 8, 1778, wishing that General's subordinate, Colonel Butler, good fortune in a contemplated attack on the Unadilla settlement of Mohawk Indians in Otsego County, New York, indicates the importance that was attached to the destruction of that place which had become a refuge for runaway slaves. There is also reference to maroon activity in the region of Shrewsbury, New Jersey, from whence it was reported in July, 1779, that about fifty escaped slaves, together with a few whites, had made off with twenty horses and eighty head of cattle.

A slave named Bill of Prince William County, Virginia, was hanged in 1781 for having led others in attacks upon plantations. Reference to similar activity is contained in a letter from Accomack County, Virginia, of September 10, 1781, by one Levin Joynes who declared: "We have had most alarming times this Summer, all along the shore, from a sett of Barges manned mostly by our own Negroes who have run off—These fellows are really dangerous to an individual singled out for their vengeance whose property lay exposed—They burnt several houses."

Letters from prominent Virginians, as Edmund Randolph and Captain John Peyton, told of the same kind of trouble in the summer of 1782. Indeed, reports of serious maroon activity, specifically stated to be due to slaves who escaped during the Revolution, persisted in Georgia and South Carolina until the year 1787.

Notwithstanding the fact that the Revolutionary period served to loosen the restraints of bondage for many thousands, by increased manumission, greater possibility of flight and, at certain times and places, enlistment in the American army and navy (the story of which will soon be told) the period had its full share of desperate attempts for freedom, of the slave's reckless, heroic protests against enslavement in the form of conspiracies and rebellions.

It would be sanguine indeed to believe that the available records furnish a complete picture of the slave plots and rebellions which occurred during the era of the Revolution (or any other) for discussion of these happenings was strictly taboo and news of them was severely censored. Yet notwithstanding the near certainty that some plots took place that escaped permanent record, and the absolute certainty that the whole truth about many of the recorded outbreaks is not available, one may still declare that existing evidence demonstrates that every year of the

Revolution saw at least one slave conspiracy or insurrection.

In the year prior to actual warfare, but during feverish agitational and organizational work, 1774, trouble among the slaves was reported from Massachusetts and Georgia. In Boston, during September, as Abigail Adams, wife of the future second President of the United States, said, there was uncovered "a conspiracy of the Negroes," which she noted, was widespread, and involved at least one white, an Irishman. Little more, however, than this is known, for, declared Mrs. Adams, the affair was "kept pretty private." In November of that same year, as the Georgia (Savannah) *Gazette* of December 7, 1774, laconically noted, there was an uprising in St. Andrew's Parish, Georgia, which resulted in the death of four whites and the wounding of three others before it was suppressed. The paper reported that two of the slave leaders suffered death by burning for daring to struggle for freedom.

The first year of warfare, 1775, witnessed several manifestations on the part of America's slaves of general discontent. The Albany, New York, Committee of Correspondence notes in a meeting of May, 1775, the presence of "Alarm arisen by suspicion of the Negroes" and in June, having observed that "meetings of Negroes are more frequent of late than usual" ordered all such gatherings forbidden, and had this order printed and widely distributed.

A very considerable conspiracy among the Negroes of Pitt, Craven, and Beaufort counties, North Carolina, was betrayed by the favorite slaves of a Captain Thomas Respess and a Mr. Dayner on July 7, 1775, one day before the rebellion was to have started. Several hundred men were immediately armed and sent scouring the country. Scores of slaves were arrested, questioned, and "a deep laid Horrid Tragic Plan" for rebellion disclosed. Dozens more were jailed (some of whom were armed, and some killed resisting arrest) and the favorite sentence seems to have been "to receive 80 lashes each (and) to have both Ears crap'd."

A resident of Craven County, one John Simpson, reported as late as July 15 that "We keep taking up, examining and scourging more or less every day." Again a white man, this time a sea captain named Johnson, was implicated in the Negroes' schemes for liberation. Finally, so far as 1775 is concerned, a letter from Charles Town, South Carolina, of August 20, makes it clear that a conspiracy to destroy the city by fire was uncovered there, and mentions that a leader of this slave plot "was hanged and burnt for intended sedition" in that city on the 19th of August.

There is proof of serious disturbance among the slaves on Tybee Island, Georgia, early in 1776, but the precise circumstances are vague. It is clear, however, that a Colonel Stephen Bull of Georgia had written to the prominent South Carolinian, Henry Laurens, about this, and Laurens' reply of March 16, 1776, contains this passage:

Now for the grand we may say awful business contained in your Letter, it is an awful business notwithstanding it has the sanction of Law, to put even fugitive and Rebellious Slaves to death—the prospect is horrible—We think the Council of Safety in Georgia ought to give that encouragement which is necessary to induce proper persons to seize and if nothing else will do to destroy all those Rebellious Negroes upon Tybee Island or wherever they may be found.

Another tantalizingly incomplete passage in an early letter offers proof of disorder among the slaves of New Jersey in the summer of 1776. In a communication from Trenton dated July 5, and written by Samuel Tucker to the President of the Continental Congress, John Hancock, is found this sentence: "The story of the Negroes may be depended upon, so far at least as to their arming and attempting to form themselves, particularly in Somerset county." Just what this attempt cost, in human terms, is not known. The slaves in the neighboring state of Pennsylvania, especially in Bucks County, gave their owners some cause for uneasiness in July, 1776, and special military precautions were taken. Nothing more definite is known, except that one of the Negroes particularly feared was named Samson and was the slave of one Jeremiah Dungan, Jr.

There is evidence of a continuous state of disaffection from January, 1777, to January, 1779, among the slaves of and around Albany County, New York (which contained over 3,800 slaves in 1771, the nearest date for which figures are available). The first year is marked by complaints of misbehavior and trials for an assault upon a soldier, while 1778, as previously noted, witnessed organized efforts to flee on the part of several slaves. Moreover, on March 11, 1778, Lafayette wrote from Albany (to the same Henry Laurens previously mentioned) of a reported plot on the part of the slaves, together with a few whites, to destroy the slave-owners and fire the city. Attempts at wholesale flight were again reported in May, 1778, and in January, 1779, a warrant was issued for the seizure of a Negro named Tom, slave of Henry Hogan for "endeavouring to Stir up the minds of the Negroes against their Masters and raising Insurrections among them." There is no record of Tom's capture.

A New York newspaper, the *Packet and American Advertiser* of July 1, 1779, gives the only information seen concerning a slave plot in New Jersey in these very few words, "On Sunday night last, it was discovered that the Negroes had it in contemplation to rise and murder the inhabitants of Elizabeth-Town. Many of them are secured in gaol." That's all.

In the fall of 1779 the British-held port of Savannah,

Georgia, was besieged, but in vain, by a combined American and French army. The British and Tories, attempting to muster all possible strength, encouraged the Negroes to aid in the fortification work and even to serve in the armed forces with promises of future emancipation. When the Revolutionary army was finally driven off, in October, the Negroes learned that liberty was not to be theirs. Then, in the words of an early historian of Georgia, William B. Stevens, "they grew bold and presumptuous." The author remarks that the danger was "great" and the "insolence" of the slaves "unbearable ... for several months" and that finally, though it "was no easy matter," they were "reduced ... to their proper obedience and position." The precise method of this process of reduction is not clear, but we may be certain it was not merely moral suasion!

Existence of trouble in Botetourt County, Virginia, early in 1780 is established by the fact that a slave named Jack was convicted there of insurrectionary activity and was sentenced, in April, to be hanged. In July of 1780 trouble matured once again in the region of Albany, New York, when several slaves, as well as two white men, William Loucks and Frederick Coonradt, were arrested for having plotted rebellion and the burning of the Half Moon settlement outside the city.

A communication from Colonel Wooding of Halifax County, Virginia, of July 21, 1781, in which an urgent appeal for more arms is made refers to fears of the slaves and Tories and notes the fact that while the planters possessed arms, they refused to part with them lest they should be unable to control their slaves. In December of 1781 the slaves in Virginia's capital, Williamsburg, set fire to several of the buildings, including that housing the government, and caused the death of one white man.

Again in Virginia, this time in Accomack County, as

appears in a letter from a Colonel Corbin of May 2, 1782, a conspiracy involving slaves and, it was said, Tories, was disclosed and suppressed. There is, finally, record of the payment by North Carolina of £50 to William Bryan of Craven County, on April 23, 1783, "for a Negro man killed in suppressing of Rebel Slaves," but it is not clear just what uprising this has reference to.

IV. SERVICE IN THE ARMED FORCES OF THE REVOLUTION

THE NAVY

Negroes, free and slave, where and when permitted to do so, played a conspicuous part in the armed forces of the Revolution. Much red tape had to be cut before the Negro, particularly the slave, was allowed to contribute his services to the Revolutionary army, but the navy, such as it was, did not, apparently, pursue a Jim-Crow policy, and there are several references to Negroes as members of the crews of the nation's infant sea fighters.

It is certain that one of the seamen aboard the Connecticut brig having the ponderous name, *Defence Colony Service,* as early as the spring of 1776, was a Negro named George. At least three Negroes, Peter, Brittain, and Daniel Peterson were in the crew of the galley *Trumbull* during the summer of 1776. On the famous Captain David Porter's privateer *Aurora* were three black seamen all known by the then common name (for Negroes) of Cato. Another named Cato fought on the brig *Julius Caesar,* and three called Cato Blackney served on the Massachusetts brigs *Hazard, Deane,* and *Prospect* during 1778 and 1779. Another Negro, named Caesar, also served aboard the *Hazard*.

A Negro named Jo Blackley and his young son Samuel were, in 1780, aboard the Massachusetts sloop *Morning Star*. Another colored youngster who served as a powder boy in this baby navy, one James Forten, was later to acquire fame and fortune as the inventor of an improved mechanism for handling sails, and an outstanding leader in the Abolitionist movement. Other Negro seamen like John Moore, Caesar Cambridge, Joshua Tiffany, Joseph Freeman, Thomas Sambo, and one listed simply as Ben's Freeman, served aboard the *Alliance, Roebuck, Confederacy, Racehorse,* and *Adventure.*

There are further scattered evidences of services rendered by Negroes to the naval forces of the Revolution. Many members of the crews who manned the defensive coastal galleys of Georgia, for example, were Negroes. A letter written by George Washington on July 26, 1779, to Major Henry Lee, also indicates the employment of Negroes, for Washington there states, "I have granted a Warrant of 1000 Dollars promised the Negro pilots." Finally, two acts of the Virginia legislature prove similar activities. That body on October 30, 1789, freed two Negroes. Jack Knight and William Boush, for having "faithfully served on board the armed vessels" of Virginia. And on November 14, 1789, it purchased the freedom of Caesar, slave of Mary Tarrant of Elizabeth City, because he had "entered very early into the service of his country, and continued to pilot the armed vessels of this state during the late war."

THE ARMY

We have all seen pictures depicting the Spirit of '76 with the gallant drummer and fifer swinging along, and other pictures of the poorly clad and under-provisioned army of Washington bleeding and shivering at Valley Forge.

But never are we told that among the Americans who stirred their comrades' spirits with drum and fife were Negroes, and that the snow of Valley Forge was reddened by black men's blood, as well as that of whites. Yet such are the facts. Concretely, for example, we know that the drummer for Captain Benjamin Egbert's company in New York City in March, 1776, was a Negro known simply as Tom. And the fifer (sometimes taking a hand at the drum, too) for Captain John Ford's company of the 27th Massachusetts regiment was Barzillai Lew, native of Groton, where he was born in 1743, and where his six-foot frame working at the trade of a cooper was a well-known sight. Barzillai Lew drummed and fifed and fought his way through the Revolutionary War from almost the moment fighting began (he enlisted May 6, 1775), down to the day, some seven years later, when the arms were stacked. Black men suffered and shivered at Valley Forge, and at least one, Phillip Field, native of Dutchess County, New York, and soldier in Captain Pelton's company of the Second New York regiment, died there in that terrible year of 1778.

Yet, as has already been noted, the existence of slavery created an embarrassing and dangerous contradiction within the Revolutionary forces. This had, as we have seen, the effect of stunting the budding Abolitionist sentiment, and it had a similar effect in producing laws and regulations to hinder the enrollment of Negroes within the ranks of the Revolutionary Army.

The Massachusetts Committee of Safety, in May, 1775, adopted a resolution sanctioning the enlistment of free Negroes, but forbidding slaves to be enrolled on the ground that such action would be "inconsistent with the principles that are to be supported, and reflect dishonor

97

on this colony." In July, 1775, both the Congress of Massachusetts and Horatio Gates, Washington's Adjutant General, issued orders against the enlistment of Negroes.

John Rutledge, a delegate from South Carolina to the Continental Congress, introduced a resolution barring Negroes from use as soldiers in September, 1775, and on October 18 this was approved by that body. Ten days before this a council of general officers of the American army had already decided unanimously against the use of slaves and, by a large majority, against the use of free Negroes as soldiers. This was followed on November 12, 1775, by George Washington's order complying with these decisions.

But now reversal of this trend began to set in. Both the legislative and military bodies observed with alarm the flocking of thousands of slaves to the British (particularly after Dunmore's proclamation of November 7, 1775), realized that every bit of man-power would be needed, and had already seen at Lexington, Concord, and Bunker Hill that the Negroes fought and fought well.

Thus George Washington issued on December 30, 1775, from his headquarters at Cambridge, Massachusetts, the following message: "As the General is informed, that Numbers of Free Negroes are desirous of inlisting, he gives leave to the recruiting Officers to entertain them, and promises to lay the matter before the Congress, who he doubts not will approve it." The next day Washington forwarded a letter to Congress telling of his action, explaining that "free Negroes who have served in this Army, are very much dissatisfied at being discarded" and that he therefore had "presumed to depart from the Resolution (of October 18, 1775), respecting them, and have given license for their being enlisted." In a resolution of January 16, 1776, the Continental Congress approved Washington's action, stating that "the free Negroes who have served faithfully in the army at Cambridge, may be re-enlisted, but no others."

Certain state regulations also affected the question of Negro service in the Revolutionary Army. New York, in 1776, permitted men who had been drafted to offer substitutes for themselves in the form of able-bodied men, white or Negro, and this led some slaveholders to offer their slaves as soldiers, the latter's reward being freedom. The Virginia act of 1776 for the organization of the militia provided that "The free mulattoes in the said companies or battalions shall be employed as drummers, fifers, or pioneers." Moreover, the act of this same state passed in May, 1777, for the purpose of completing the troop quota contained this very interesting passage:

And whereas several Negro slaves have deserted from their masters, and under pretence of being free men have enlisted as soldiers: For prevention whereof, Be it enacted, that it shall not be lawful for any recruiting officer within this commonwealth to enlist any Negro or mulatto into the service of this or either of the United States, until such Negro or mulatto shall produce a certificate from some justice of the peace for the county wherein he resides that he is a feee man.

In February, 1778, Rhode Island, and in April, 1778, Massachusetts, finding the going getting tougher, the man-supply thinning, and the slaves as willing as ever to fight —provided they received their freedom—passed laws for the enrollment of slaves as soldiers in their state forces. Several hundred Negroes in this way became free. An incidental phrase in a North Carolina law of 1778, passed for the purpose of wiping out the problem of runaway slaves (in which, of course, it failed) demonstrates the fact that Negroes were serving in the army of that state. For this law in making provisions for the capture and disposal of fugitives adds, "nothing herein contained shall deprive of Liberty any Slave who having been liberated & not

99

sold by order of any Court has inlisted in the service of this or the United States."

It is to be noted that strenuous efforts were made in 1778 and 1779 to persuade South Carolina and Georgia to permit the enrollment of Negroes as soldiers, but these never succeeded (never formally, at any rate, though, as we shall see, Negroes from those states did serve in the Revolutionary Army). Behind this move were prominent individuals like Henry Laurens, Alexander Hamilton, James Madison, Generals Lincoln and Greene and even, though not quite wholeheartedly, George Washington. Indeed, the Continental Congress in March, 1779, adopted a resolution urging Georgia and South Carolina, for the sake of saving the cause in those regions, to permit the enlistment of three thousand Negroes (with Congress paying $1,000 for each Negro who would, of course, then be free) but both these states shuddered at the proposition and even hinted that they would withdraw from the struggle before acceding to this request. (It may incidentally be noted that, largely because of the great slave population and this reactionary attitude, nearly all of Georgia and eastern South Carolina were conquered and controlled by the British.)

Maryland in October, 1780, and again in May, 1781, passed laws permitting Negroes, slave and free, to be recruited into its armed forces. And finally, the State of New York, in accordance with an act of March 20, 1781, raised two regiments of slaves all of whom were enlisted with the understanding that faithful service for the duration of the war would bring liberty.

The fact of the widespread presence of Negroes in the first armies of the United States is established by the laws and resolutions which have been enumerated. Other evidence in the form of eyewitness accounts also demonstrates how numerous these Negroes were.

A Southern rifleman, for instance, in the ranks of the Continental forces near Boston wrote, in September, 1775, concerning that People's Army, "Such Sermons, such Negroes, such Colonels, such Boys, and such Great Great Grandfathers." Again, a rather aristocratic and wealthy young Pennsylvanian, Alexander Graydon, who served in 1775 in the same army, deprecated its poor discipline and went on to declare, "The only exception I recollect to have seen, to these miserably constituted bands from New England, was the regiment of (John) Glover from Marblehead (Massachusetts). There was an appearance of discipline in this corps. . . . But even in this regiment there were a number of Negroes, which, to persons unaccustomed to such associations, had a disagreeable, degrading effect."

A letter written by a Hessian officer, Schloezer, in the service of George III, on October 23, 1777, referred, by implication at least, to the disagreeable effect, of another kind, that the presence of these Negro soldiers produced when it declared that "no regiment [among the Americans] is to be seen in which there are not Negroes in abundance and among them are able-bodied, strong, and brave fellows."

References to specific Negroes who performed particularly valiant deeds, and references to specific battles in which the presence of Negroes was marked often occur and prove the important role they played in winning the independence of the United States. Occasionally, too, has come down to us note of the wounding or killing of particular Negroes in certain battles.

The pension lists of the State of Pennsylvania, for example, mention a Negro named John Francis who served in Captain Epple's company of the Third Pennsylvania Regiment and who "had both legs much shattered by grape shot at Battle of Brandywine on 11th of Sept. 1777." A

Negro known merely as London was killed in the combined British and Indian siege of Boonesborough, in what is now Kentucky, in 1778. When the British, led by the traitor Benedict Arnold, stormed Fort Griswold on September 6, 1781, and massacred the defenders, two Negroes, Jordan Freeman, who before dying managed to kill the British Major Montgomery, and Lambert Latham, were among those killed, the latter with over thirty wounds in his body. On the bloody field of Eutaw in South Carolina on September 8, 1781, were found the bodies of an unnamed Negro soldier of the Maryland line and a British soldier each transfixed by the bayonet of the other. Again, in the decisive siege of Cornwallis at Yorktown, Virginia, in October, 1781, a Rhode Island Negro, Bristol Rhodes, lost a leg and an arm. Finally, in the last organized effort of the war, the futile march from Saratoga to (it was intended) the British forces at Oswego, New York, in the midst of a fierce winter in February, 1783, Negro soldiers formed the bulk of the American force that was, perhaps by treachery, led off its course, and dozens died or were maimed by freezing.

Negroes were present, too, in the earliest battles of the war. Among those at Lexington and Concord in April, 1775, firing the shots "heard around the world" were, at least, the following Negroes: Caesar Ferrit and his son John of Natick, Samuel Craft of Newton, Peter Salem of Framingham, Pomp Blackman of points unspecified, and Lemuel Haynes, native of West Hartford, Connecticut, and destined to be a famous theologian and minister for white congregations in New England (and, at long last, to have his portrait displayed, in November, 1939, in the museum at Bennington, Vermont).

Many Negroes were present at the never-to-be-forgotten Battle of Bunker Hill of June 17, 1775, and at least one of them, Caesar Brown of Westford, Massachusetts, was there killed in action. The giant cooper, fifer, and drummer, Barzillai Lew, whom we have already met, was present. A Negro named Robin from Sandown, New Hampshire, was there, too, as were the Massachusetts Negroes, Pomp Fisk, Prince Hall, later a pioneer leader in the Negro Masonic movement as well as in the Abolitionist movement, Titus Colburn, Cuff Hayes, Caesar Dickerson, Cato Tufts, Caesar Weatherbee, Seymour Burr, Grant Cooper, Charlestown Eads, Sampson Talbert, Caesar Basom, Salem Poor and Peter Salem. It was the last named who killed the first Englishman to mount the American breastworks, Major Pitcairn—he who had led the British at Lexington.

And the gallantry of Salem Poor was so conspicuous on this occasion that, on December 5, 1775, it was formally called to the attention of the Massachusetts legislature. This commendation was signed by fourteen officers including Lieutenant Colonel Thomas Nixon and Colonels Jonathan Brewer and William Prescott (he who had flashed the words, "Don't fire until you see the whites of their eyes"), and declared that Salem Poor had, under fire, "behaved like an experienced officer, as well as an excellent soldier. To set forth particulars of his conduct would be tedious...in the person of this said Negro centres a brave and gallant soldier."

Negroes were present, too, in the first aggressive action of the American forces, the capturing of Fort Ticonderoga on May 10, 1775. It was cannon captured here by Ethan Allen's Green Mountain Boys and dragged down to Washington's army facing Boston that finally forced the British to evacuate that port. At that important battle were Lemuel Haynes and two native Vermont Negro members of the Green Mountain Boys, Primas Black and Epheram Blackman.

Scores of other Negroes from Vermont and New Hampshire served in the militia throughout the war, during border forays, attacks on villages and American advances into Canada. As examples, for Vermont may be mentioned Cato Negor, Prince Freeman, Hallam Blackmer, Solomon Scipio, Mingo Black; and for New Hampshire, Fortune Negro, Benajah Blackman, John Blackman, Titus Freeman, Moody Freeman, John Freeman, Mark Blackey, Cesar Black, Titus Willson, Scipio Brown, William Sharper, John Reed, Asa Purham, George Black, Jude Hall, Gloster Watson, Sidon Martin, Jubil Martin, and many listed simply as Peter, Zach, Richard, Cato, George, Corridon, Paul, Oxford, Oliver, Primas, Dan, Prince, Archelus, and Fortunatus.

In addition to the battles already mentioned—Concord, Lexington, Ticonderoga, Bunker Hill, Brandywine, Boonesborough (1778), Fort Griswold, Eutaw, Yorktown, the attempt at Oswego—definite evidence exists proving the presence of Negroes, as American fighters, at the battles of White Plains, Long Island, Stillwater, Bennington, Red Bank, Bemis Heights, Saratoga, Stony Point, Fort George, Savannah, Rhode Island, Trenton, Princeton, Monmouth, Boonesborough (1780), and Bryan's Station. Of these struggles Negroes were particularly prominent, from the viewpoint of numbers, at Long Island, Red Bank, Rhode Island, Savannah, and the terrible fight at Monmouth, on June 28, 1778, when the treachery of America's first ranking Major-General, Charles Lee, almost brought disaster to the entire Revolutionary cause. The day was saved only by the combined efforts of Wayne, Steuben and Washington, and the stubborn grit and splendid heroism of their men, black and white (together with the woman, Molly Pitcher).

Mention of this white lady, Molly Pitcher, brings to mind the fact that she has been made (quite properly, of course) a national heroine because of her pluck in servicing a cannon on that June day of 1778 after her husband

104

had been disabled. But, significantly enough, practically nothing is said of a Negro lady, Deborah Gannett, who served as a regular soldier, under the name of Robert Shurtliff, in the Fourth Massachusetts Regiment of the Continental Army, not for one day but for some seventeen months, from May 20, 1782, to October 23, 1783. The State of Massachusetts granted this remarkable woman a reward of £34 on January 20, 1792, and declared, on doing this, that "the said Deborah exhibited an extraordinary instance of female heroism."

Other outstanding exploits are worth special mention. Two of the soldiers selected by Washington to take part in the daring crossing of the Delaware River on Christmas Day, 1776, preparatory to the surprise attack upon the Hessians at Trenton, were the Negroes Oliver Cromwell and Prince Whipple, the latter of whom was in the commander's own boat. Again, of the forty-one men and officers selected by Lieutenant Colonel William Barton to take part in the surprise raid on the British headquarters at Newport, Rhode Island, on July 9, 1777, one was a Negro, Tack Sisson. And, after having overcome the guards, the Negro soldier was one of the few who crashed into the building housing the British General Richard Prescott, and captured both that officer and Major Barrington, and succeeded in bringing both back to the American lines, thus performing one of the most amazing deeds of the American Revolution.

In the allied American and French siege of Savannah in 1779 the French forces included about seven hundred Haitian free Negroes formed in what was known as the Fontages Legion. The allied forces lost over eleven hundred men (including the heroic Pole, Pulaski) and were well-nigh annihilated in a sudden attack of a British force under Lieutenant Colonel Maitland. But this onslaught was met by the Fontages Legion and in, as was said, "the most brilliant feat of the day" these Negroes repulsed the British attack and permitted the Americans to carry out an orderly retreat. Many of these black fighters carried the Revolutionary seed back to their homeland and were important in establishing the Haitian Republic. Among them were Christophe, who was wounded in this battle, and was destined to be the successor of Toussaint L'Ouverture; and Andre, Beauvais, Rigaud, Villatte, Beauregard, and Lambert, each of whom was to rise to high rank in the fight for Haitian liberation.

The feats of Francis Marion, the guerrilla fighter of South Carolina, have long been celebrated, but rarely is it mentioned that among his original group of fighters were Negroes. Late in the war other Negroes, under Barzillai Lew (the same one!) carried on an anti-British guerrilla warfare in New England.

There were, also, several companies formed exclusively of Negroes, as that composed of Massachusetts Negroes and commanded by a white man named Samuel Lawrence, and that formed by Connecticut Negroes (four of whom were named Liberty, and three named Freedom) under Colonel Humphreys, and that formed by Rhode Island Negroes under Colonel Olney. In addition, there was one company of Massachusetts Negroes, called "The Bucks of America," which was Negro right up to and including the commander, one Middleton. Moreover, record of at least one Negro officer, in a mixed company, has been discovered in the person of a corporal named Perley Rogers in the Second Massachusetts Regiment commanded by Colonel John Bailey.

It may, indeed, be declared that Negroes from every state fought in the ranks of the Revolutionary army. As a matter of fact, in the case of a few states, like Maryland, New York, Connecticut, Rhode Island, Massachusetts, and New Hampshire, one would have difficulty in naming many hamlets, villages, or cities from which some Negro soldier did not enlist.

A good example of this is the State of Connecticut (which contained about 6,500 Negroes in 1774) whose records were especially well-kept, and show Negro volunteers from at least forty-seven different localities within that state, from Ashford to Woodstock, from Branford to Woodbury, from Canaan to Winchester. There is, even for the State of Georgia, positive proof that at least five Negroes from that region fought against the British, these being Daniel Cresswell, John Maffett, Hugh Hall, one simply named Wood, and Austin Dabney. The last named was not only freed for his particularly courageous behavior, having conducted himself "with a bravery and fortitude which would have honored a freeman," but was awarded an annual pension of ninety-six dollars and given one hundred and twelve acres of land. At least one South Carolina Negro, John Eady, also distinguished himself in the Revolutionary Army and likewise received his freedom and land.

A final piece of evidence concerning Negroes in the Revolutionary army appears in a very interesting enactment passed by the Virginia legislature in October, 1783. It is self-explanatory and reads: "Whereas it hath been represented to the general assembly that during the course of the war many persons in this state had caused their slaves to enlist in certain regiments or corps raised within the same, having tendered such slaves to the officers appointed to recruit forces within the state, as substitutes for free persons, whose lot or duty it was to serve in such regiments or corps, at the same time representing to such recruiting officers that the slaves so enlisted by their direction and concurrence were freemen; and it appearing further to this assembly, that on the expiration of the term of enlistment of such slaves that the former owners have attempted again to force them to return to a state of servitude, contrary to the principles of justice, and to their own solemn promise," and since, said Virginia, such Negroes, by their service, "have thereby of course contributed towards the establishment of American liberty and independence," the Attorney General of the state was instructed to see to it that those Negroes remained free.

In summing up this phase of the story one may say in full confidence that the number of Negroes who served as regular soldiers in the American forces during the Revolution was, at a conservative estimate, five thousand, to which may be added the approximately seven hundred Negroes who fought in the ranks of this country's French ally.

THE NEGROES AS SPIES

Nor does that complete the account of the direct aid given by the Negro people to this cause, for excellent evidence exists proving that Negroes were at times invaluable in the capacity of spies. An unnamed Negro, for example, was largely responsible for the American victory at Edenton, North Carolina, on December 8, 1775, when Colonel Woodford defeated a British force under Captain Fordyce, suffering himself the loss of but one man while accounting for one hundred redcoats. This occurred because a Negro had, under Colonel Woodford's orders, entered the British camp and told, in such a convincing fashion, of a weak, disorganized American force, that the English hastily attacked what in reality was a well-prepared and strategically placed American force. Of this engagement, incidentally, the late historian, William E. Dodd, wrote, "It was a godsend to the revolutionists of Virginia; it stirred drooping spirits as they had not been stirred since the news of Lexington."

Anthony Wayne's surprise attack upon and rather easy

capture of the Stony Point, New York fort, in July, 1779, was made possible by the spying activity of a Negro slave, Pompey, property of an American, Captain Lamb. Pompey, whose invaluable activity here gained him his freedom, obtained the British password, and used this in aiding a detachment of Americans to overcome the British guards, thus leading to the surprise and seizure of the stronghold together with considerable supplies and six hundred prisoners.

Rhode Island, in 1782, freed a Negro, Quaco Honeyman, as a reward for his important spying activity, and South Carolina in 1783 freed the wife and child of a deceased Negro whose efforts in that direction had also been valuable. Virginia, in 1786, freed James, slave of William Armistead, because he had, in 1781, as the act of emancipation declares, entered "into the service of the Marquis la Fayette, and at the peril of his life found means to frequent the British camp, and thereby faithfully executed important commissions entrusted to him by the marquis." The same state in 1792 freed another Negro, Saul, property of a George Kelly, for certain unspecified "very essential services rendered to the Commonwealth during the late war."

V. CONCLUSION

We have attempted to show that the activities of a homogeneous one-fifth of the population of the United States during her first Revolution were varied and important and must be understood if one is fully to comprehend not only this vital phase of the Negro's history, but also the American Revolution itself.

All the manifold efforts of these five hundred thousand people—their court actions and petitions, their conspiracies and uprisings, their flight and guerrilla warfare, their service in the infant nation's navy and army as pilots, seamen, soldiers, and spies—had as their fundamental motivation the achievement of equality and liberty, the full realization, in practice, of the Declaration of Independence.

It has been shown that some very definite advances in this direction were made, particularly in the North, during the Revolution, and that this, together with service in the armed forces, did lead to the liberation of several thousand slaves. Yet it was demonstrated that the movement fell short, was compromised, and that because of this tens of thousands of slaves felt impelled to seek freedom by flight or rebellion. It must, moreover, be declared that this failure came close to bringing victory to the English, and that it is probable the British would indeed have won had not their own position made it impossible for them to wage a really thoroughgoing war of liberation.

It appears, also, safe to say that the failure to carry out fully the freeing of the Negro people led to the postponement for many bloody months of the final victory of the American forces. And it is certain that the failure to root out this cancer of slavery from the body of America led, in less than eighty years, to a most sanguinary Civil War, and required the loss of half a million lives before the second American Revolution could complete the task neglected by the first.

THE NEGRO IN THE ABOLITIONIST
MOVEMENT

I. INTRODUCTION

The crusade against the institution of Negro slavery in the United States has received two dominant types of treatment. Yet these have one thing in common: both "forget" the Negro.

One group is made up of chauvinistic, reactionary writers like Ralph V. Harlow, Avery Craven, and Arthur Y. Lloyd, who damn the Abolitionists (white people in every case) as mischievous fanatics, at best. More generally they denounce them as knaves who attacked with lies and falsehoods a lovely, patriarchal civilization, and who thus "forced" the slaveholders to defend that civilization.

These normally aloof academicians become exceedingly heated when they contemplate the Abolitionist movement, for they vaguely grasp the revolutionary implications of that struggle. It had as its aim the overthrow of a vested interest representing billions of dollars' worth of private property, and the realization in life of the Declaration of Independence, with its promise of equality and brotherhood for millions of dark-skinned people whose condition had made a mockery of that declaration. Such anti-Abolitionist writers must be aware that the fight against chattel slavery was but one battle in man's everlasting struggle for independence, justice, and peace; they know that this was a prelude to the next battle which, in the words of Wendell Phillips, one of the leading Abolitionists, was to be "that between the working class and the money kings." Realizing in effect their own alignment with reaction, they deride and slander and falsify the valiant efforts made a few generations ago by American men and women,

Negro and white, to destroy the greatest immediate obstacle then existing to the forward march of humanity; namely, the institution of slavery under which men owned those who were their workers.

The other group, to which belong historians like Albert B. Hart, Gilbert H. Barnes, and Dwight L. Dumond, writes from a liberal, humanitarian angle. The revolutionary implications of the Abolitionist movement are not too clear for these historians, yet they do recognize the brutality and ugliness of slavery and so cannot help but admire those who aided in its destruction. Characteristically, however, they fail to consider the vital importance of the Negro people in breaking their own chains, both by independent work and by work within and through mixed groups.

Because of these authors the Abolitionist movement has been dealt with, when at all sympathetically considered, as a white man's benevolent association. The Negro, when mentioned, has been presented as an alms-taking, passive, humble, meek individual. A striking illustration of this appeared in a recent work by Professor Dwight L. Dumond.* The reader will search the index of that book in vain for the name of a single Negro. He will find there mention of comparatively obscure white anti-slavery people, like Edward Weed and Calvin Waterbury, Hiram Foote and Augustus Wattles, but Frederick Douglass, Harriet Tubman, Henry Highland Garnet, David Ruggles, William Wells Brown, Samuel E. Cornish, Robert Purvis, Richard Allen, David Walker and Sojourner Truth and literally scores more, the activities of any one of whom were infinitely more important than the combined labors of the other four, receive not a word.

Negro scholars themselves, above all the distinguished

* Dwight L. Dumond, *Anti-slavery Origins of the Civil War in the United States,* University of Michigan Press, Ann Arbor, Michigan.

historian, Dr. Carter G. Woodson, have done much to uncover the truth concerning the vital role of their forebears in this crusade. But even here the work has been largely of a scattered, piecemeal, isolated nature, lacking significant details and, above all, synthesis. It is, however, true that the great body of pioneering spade work has been accomplished, often in spite of severe obstacles, by Negro investigators.

Full glory is to be granted to the dauntless white men and women, William L. Garrison and Susan B. Anthony, Theodore D. Weld and Elizabeth C. Stanton, John Brown and Prudence Crandall, Charles Sumner and Lucretia Mott, who braved the derision of the press and pulpit, faced the taunts and blows of the "respectable" mobs, tasted the abominations of nineteenth-century prisons rather than cease the struggle for the liberation of millions of Negroes in chains. There is no desire to lessen their just claim on our admiration.

But to overlook or neglect in this battle the Negro soldiers who filled these prisons; who felt the whip's lash on their backs; built the Underground Railroad and were its passengers; organized societies long before the American Anti-Slavery Society was born and published newspapers years before the *Liberator* appeared, and made possible by active support and aid both that society and that newspaper—to "forget" all this is as absurd and erroneous as it would be to "forget" Washington, Jefferson, and Sam Adams in writing the history of the American Revolution.

Let us then, briefly, investigate the role of the Negro in the epic contest against human bondage which forms one of the greatest chapters in the history of the United States.

II. APOLOGETICS OF SLAVOCRACY

There were two main deceits upon which rested the apologetics for the institution of slavery. On the one hand it was asserted that the system was an eminently beneficial one, with ease, contentment, and happiness as characteristic of the laboring population. And on the other hand it was asserted that the people who were enslaved were innately inferior to their masters and so their condition represented merely the adaptation in practice of a position predetermined by nature and by God. Thus, in the words of a young slaveholder, "if it could be proved that Negroes are more than a link between man and brute, the rest follows of course, and he must liberate all his."

These basic frauds could be and were most effectively combated only by the Negro people themselves. Contented, were they? Merry in their misery? Delighting in their degradation? If so, whence came these furtive, fleeting figures, half starved and in tatters, forcing their way into every corner of the nation and into Canada and into Mexico? Is it perhaps not true, then, that they came in large numbers to our little Salem, Ohio, or Rochester, New York, or Chester, Pennsylvania, or Worcester, Massachusetts, from Maryland or Virginia or South Carolina or Alabama? Did they or did they not actually walk or crawl or swim those 300 or 600 or 1,200 miles, confining themselves to the untracked and unmarked forests and wastelands like so many hunted beasts, advertised for like so many stray cattle? We know that they did. Theodore Weld wrote of one who reached New York in 1838: "He has come 1,200 miles from the lower part of Alabama, traveling only at night, feeding on roots and wild berries. He swam *every river* between Tuscaloosa and Pennsylvania."

And is it not true that others among these supposed felicitous inhabitants of a patriarchal paradise fled away to congregate in the swamps and mountains of the South and form their own communities, do their own farming, stand off raiding parties, wage guerrilla warfare? We know that they did; and here are the slaveholders' own newspapers to prove it: the Wilmington *Chronicle* in July, 1795, the Raleigh *Register* in June, 1802, and November, 1818, the Edenton *Gazette* in October, 1811, and May, 1820, the Charleston *City Gazette* in October, 1823, the Norfolk *Herald* in May and June, 1823, the Mobile *Register* in June, 1827, the Louisiana *Advertiser* in June, 1836, the New Orleans *Picayune* in July, 1837, the New Orleans *Bee* in October, 1841, the Hanesville *Free Press* in March, 1844, the Vicksburg *Whig* in May, 1857, the Norfolk *Day Book* in October, 1859. Did these communities become so numerous that state militia units and even United States Army troops with heavy cannon were sent against them? Yes, time and again, as in Florida in 1816, South' Carolina in 1816, North Carolina in 1821 and Virginia in 1823.

And whence come these reports that every so often pierce thick veils of censorship, of conspiracies and rebellions, on sea and land, of slave-created fires and slave-poisoned food? Who are these Gabriels and Peters and Veseys and Turners and Toms and Catos and their thousands of fellow conspirators and insurrectionists? What of the victims of punitive reprisals whose seared flesh perfumes South Carolina's air, whose swaying bodies ornament Louisana's scenery? Are these the quondam meek, contented, docile people of whom we have heard a word or two? Something of the effect of these things is indi-

117

cated in these words of an influential contemporary, Horace Greeley, written in 1856:

Here we have amid all the nonsense about the contented condition of the slave, amid all the lovely Southside portraits of the institution, accounts of a widespread conspiracy—how widespread we know not—in different states, ready to rush forth and deluge the country in blood, evoke a war of mutual extermination, and call for northern interference.

III. THE EXTENSION OF THE STRUGGLE

The last phrase in this quotation brings up another vital factor behind the growth of the Abolitionist movement that flowed, in large part, from the activities of the slaves themselves; namely, the nationalizing of the institution and its instruments of suppression, the inevitable broadening of the struggle for equality and liberty for the Negro people into one to preserve and extend the rights and freedom of all other Americans.

In order to maintain the institution of human bondage it was necessary to identify the institution with patriotism and the entire social order, and to shun as pariahs and finally to condemn as criminals all who questioned the validity of that identification. The slave-owning class did this first within its own bailiwick so that in the South any sort of freedom—of speech, press, religion, petition, assembly—was a shadow, a name and, with some, a dream. But more was needed to maintain and strengthen that institution than the stultification of the original territory claimed for slavery. It became necessary, or it was declared to be necessary, to expand the bounds of slavery so that on the one hand areas of refuge for fleeing slaves and centers from which disaffection was spread might be destroyed, and on the other so that the density of the slave population within a restricted area might not become so great as to make the control of that population impossible. These considerations were important, to cite but a few examples, in this nation's acquisition of West and East Florida and Texas, and even in a Southern sponsored exploratory trip into the Amazon Valley.

Again, it was necessary to prevent the flight of slaves, and, above all, when that was impossible to recapture those who had fled, so that the practice might not spread so widely as to endanger the institution itself. For this two things were important: first, regulatory measures to control the Negroes, and, second, penalizing measures for those who aided them.

Important, too, was the suppression of articulate anti-slavery sentiment in the nation as a whole as had been done in the South. Let anti-slavery presses be destroyed or boycotted, anti-slavery assemblies broken up or forbidden, anti-slavery agitators stoned and jailed, anti-slavery petitions treated with contempt and disdain. (The Congress of the United States actually tabled the Declaration of Independence, because of its implicit anti-slavery sentiments, when presented as a petition from American citizens!) Negro seamen were dangerous and could not be allowed to leave their ships, under threat of imprisonment, when in the harbors of the Southern states. If Great Britain protested that such action was harmful to certain of her nationals, that was just too bad; and if Massachusetts also protested and sent a distinguished son, Judge Samuel Hoar, to plead personally for fair treatment to her citizens, that, too, was just too bad. The venerable judge himself was in fact compelled to flee for his life. And, notwithstanding the myriad devices of repression developed within the South, the slaveholders felt it advisable to have the armed forces of the Federal government always available, and these were on several occasions used as either slave-catching agencies or for purposes of suppression.

These things, stemming from the activities of the Negro people, put many pregnant questions before the minds of all Americans: Shall our tax money go to support an armed force used to suppress efforts at liberation? Shall we pay magistrates for the "service" of returning men and women to slavery? Shall we ourselves refuse the call of those who come to our doors hungry and in tatters? Shall we turn them away empty handed? Shall we even lend a hand in capturing these fugitives? And if we do feed and clothe and shelter these men and women and children, are we indeed criminals subject to fine and imprisonment? And may not my neighbor, may not I, speak our mind on this subject, write what we please, read what we wish? Is our country always to be a byword and an abomination in the four corners of the earth? Shall we on July 4 praise liberty and equality and on three hundred and sixty-four other days deny both to millions of our fellows?

The poison of racism received quantities of antidotes from the work of the Negroes themselves; it was not only the magnificent personages prominent in the Abolitionist movement itself who were important cleansing agents. In the birth struggle of the republic had fought some four or five thousand Negroes. They too had crossed the Delaware, shivered at Valley Forge, stormed Stony Point, bled at Monmouth, besieged Savannah, trapped Cornwallis. The farmers of western Massachusetts who rallied under Shays against the aristocrats and parasites of the East had selected "Moses Sash of Worthington . . . a Negro man and Laborer" to be "a Captain and one of Shays' Council."

Every sixth man in the navy that held its own against the ships of England in the War of 1812 was a Negro, and of them Commodore Stephen Decatur had said: "They are as brave men as ever fired a gun. There are no stouter hearts in the service." Among those who held off veterans of Wellington's campaigns in New Orleans were scores of Negroes, and their courage won the unstinted praise of their commander, Andrew Jackson.

The achievements of many Negroes in the ante-bellum years gave the lie to the ethnological prop of bourbon theory. Thus Henry Blair, a Maryland Negro, invented machines for harvesting corn and James Forten of Philadelphia (a leader in the anti-slavery fight) invented an improved device for handling sails, while the sugar-refining industry was revolutionized by the evaporating pan conceived by Norbert Rillieux, a Louisiana Negro. As early as the eighteenth century the medical knowledge of the Negro, James Derham, had attracted such national attention that the eminent Dr. Benjamin Rush devoted an article to his work. In the nineteenth century several Negroes, notwithstanding great difficulties, won recognition as excellent physicians, among them James McCune Smith, Martin Delany, James Ulett, Peter Ray, John De Grasse, and David P. Jones. Dentists, too, like James McCrummell, Joseph Wilson, and Thomas Kennard, and noted lawyers like Robert Morris, Malcolm B. Allen, and George B. Vashon appeared. Excellent mathematicians, like Benjamin Banneker (who helped survey the site for the city of Washington), theologians like Lemuel Haynes, poets like Phyllis Wheatley, George Moses Horton, and Frances E. Harper, actors like Ira Aldridge, artists like Patrick Reason and Robert S. Duncanson contributed to the national culture.

And they disturbed the nation's conscience. For every new device these people conceived, every sick person they restored to health, every case they argued, every sermon delivered, every poem published, every play performed, and every painting executed served to refute the stereotyped view of the Negro people, the existence of which was so important for the slaveholders. It made many people realize that a system, which attempted to degrade a people who, overcoming such barriers, could produce such figures, was wrong and evil and should be destroyed.

Other activities of the Negro people more directly connected with the anti-slavery struggle, but still not part of an organized Abolitionist movement, were important in furthering the cause. Notable among these were the efforts made by Negroes to accumulate enough money to buy freedom for themselves and others near and dear to them. In this way thousands broke away from slavery and many were able actively to enter the field of anti-slavery work. Moreover, the practice itself was a telling blow at the entire ideological base of the system. It evoked the appreciative tribute of persons like Theodore Weld, the Abolitionist, who observed it in action. When he was in Cincinnati in 1834, he discovered that about 75 per cent of the three thousand Negroes in that city had "worked out their own freedom," and that many among them were "toiling to purchase their friends" still in bondage. Said Weld:

I visited this week about thirty families and found that some members of more than half of these families were still in bondage, and the father, mother, and children were struggling to lay up money enough to purchase their freedom. I found one man who had just finished paying for his wife and five children. Another man and wife had bought themselves some years ago and have been working night and day to buy their children; they had just redeemed the last and had paid for themselves and children $1,400! Another woman had recently paid the last installment of the purchase money for her husband. She had purchased him by taking in washing and working late at night, after going out and performing as help at hard work. But I cannot tell half, and must stop. After spending three or four hours and getting facts, I was forced to stop from sheer heartache and agony.

Some Negroes combined public tours with personal labor in an effort to raise the ransom money, thus bringing the subject of slavery to the doors of thousands of citizens who had hitherto viewed it as a matter which in no way concerned them. Thus, Peter Still obtained his liberty and that of his wife and three children at a total cost of $5,500, a sum raised in three years by his own work and by speeches delivered throughout New England, New York, and Pennsylvania. Lunsford Lane of North Carolina similarly obtained the freedom of himself, his wife, and seven children (at a cost of $3,500), by making speeches chiefly in Massachusetts and Ohio. As a final example may be mentioned Noah Davis, a shoemaker of Fredericksburg, Virginia, who was able to raise $4,000 with which to purchase his own freedom and that of his wife and five children by twelve years of persistent toil, as well as by making public appeals in New York, Pennsylvania, and Massachusetts.

In the words of Levi Coffin, the Quaker, these pleas were "hard to refuse, almost impossible if one brought the case home to himself." They were heard one day in 1849 by James Russell Lowell and, though short of funds, he could not resist "such an appeal," for "if a man comes and asks us to help him buy a wife or child, what are we to do?" The cry of a son—"Help me *buy my mother!*" and the cry of a mother—"Help me *buy my children!*" were not easily denied or quickly forgotten, and they rang in the ears of many Americans a few generations ago, causing a host to vow that such exhortations must cease.

Of greater significance, however, than the efforts to

buy freedom—indeed, probably the most important single item in the entire anti-slavery crusade—was the flight northward of tens of thousands of slaves. This brought the staunchest, most unswerving, and most dramatic individuals into the organized Abolitionist movement. The flight of these slaves produced a keen feeling of insecurity among the slaveowners and thus moved them to severe acts of restriction which, in turn, aroused great opposition to slavery. The very appearance of numerous living testimonials to the "joys" of the patriarchal system, the very act, on the part of Negro and white, of offering the fugitives food and shelter and advice (which through repetition grew into the Underground Railroad system) had a tremendous effect in producing and developing anti-slavery feeling.

No people anywhere in the world have shown greater ingenuity and heroism than have the American Negro people in their efforts to flee the land of sorrow. First come the heroes who started out, often knowing no more than that somewhere North was freedom, with no guide but the North star, no road but the forest and swamp, seeing in every white person a probable enemy, and leaving behind folks whom they loved. They went; thousands of them. Many failed, died in the attempt or were recaptured and suffered lashes or were sold again.

But others succeeded,* and their success was made possible originally by the aid of other Negroes, free and slave, an assistance given in spite of the heavy penalties involved. Ship stewards, railroad workers, and teamsters among the Negroes in the southern communities were of great importance in this regard. Several, like Leonard Grimes in Richmond and Samuel D. Burris in Wilmington, were sentenced to many years' imprisonment. Some

* At least sixty thousand fugitive slaves reached the North from 1830 to 1860.

idea of how widespread this activity was appears from the fact that out of eighty-one free Negroes in the Richmond penitentiary in 1848 ten were serving sentences for the "crime" of aiding or abetting slaves to escape from their masters.

Once beyond the Mason and Dixon line, particularly until about 1835, Negroes again were outstanding, and almost alone, in assisting the fugitives either to find a region within the United States that was relatively safe, or to get into Canada where protection from re-enslavement was practically certain. Thus the Quaker, Levi Coffin, whose splendid service for fugitive slaves over a period of some thirty years earned him the title of president of the Underground Railroad, testified that when he left North Carolina and settled in Newport, Indiana, in 1826 he observed that "fugitives often passed through that place and generally stopped among the colored people." He then offered to assist in this work and so entered upon his career as a leading deliverer of human property. Indeed, as late as 1837 James G. Birney made a similar observation while in Cincinnati. He learned that two fugitive slaves, a man and wife, had recently passed through the town, and that they had been cared for by Negroes. This, he remarked, was typical, since "such matters are almost uniformly managed by the colored people. I know nothing of them generally till they are past."

Later, as the Abolitionist movement grew and expanded and the rails of the Underground Railroad branched through hundreds of homes in scores of communities, embracing thousands of workers on the road, Negroes remained prominent among them. Among those who led in the movement were William Still in Philadelphia, David Ruggles in New York, Stephen Myers in Albany, Frederick Douglass in Rochester, Lewis Hayden in Boston, J. W. Loguen in Syracuse, Martin R. Delany in

Pittsburgh, George De Baptist in Madison, Indiana, John Hatfield in Cincinnati, William Goodrich in York, Pennsylvania, Stephen Smith, William Whipper, and Thomas Bessick in Columbia, Pennsylvania, Daniel Ross and John Augusta in Norristown, Pennsylvania, Samuel Bond in Baltimore, Sam Nixon in Norfolk. There were others known only by pseudonyms such as William Penn, and Ham and Eggs, while still others were referred to simply as "a ferryman on the Susquehanna" or "an old seamstress in Baltimore."

This railroad did not have only stationary agents, for some went into the South "to drum up business," that is, to bring the message to the slaves that there were people anxious to see them free and ready to help them escape. Some of the individuals who undertook this exceedingly dangerous work were white people, like Alexander M. Ross, James Redpath, William L. Chaplin, Charles Torrey, Calvin Fairbanks, and Delia Webster. Among these agitators the best known was John Brown, who undertook this activity on the urgings of a Missouri slave known only as Jim. In December, 1858, having just recovered from typhoid fever, he and a few comrades led by Jim went from Kansas into Missouri, freed ten slaves, killed a resisting slaveholder, and headed north. Though outlawed, pursued by posses, and with a reward on his head offered by the President of the United States, John Brown led his courageous band of men and women through Kansas, Nebraska, Iowa, Illinois, and Michigan into Canada, where he left them in March of 1859.

But the vast majority of those who "carried the war into Africa" were Negroes, the names of a few of whom are known, like Josiah Henson, William Still, Elijah Anderson, John Mason, and, above all, that heroic woman, Harriet Tubman. About the latter, who was known to her people as Moses, John Brown said in his laconic way that she was "the most of a man, naturally, that I ever met with." She made trip after trip from the land of slavery to the land of freedom, personally leading over three hundred human beings on the long and weary trek from bondage to liberty. Though engaged in this work for years, and with heavy rewards offered for her capture, dead or alive, she was never taken. She served as nurse, spy and guerrilla fighter through the course of the Civil War. Her death on March 10, 1913, in Auburn, New York, closed an almost incredible life wholly devoted to the emancipation of her people.

There were many others who took part in this work; it has been estimated that in 1860 about five hundred Negroes from Canada alone went into the South to rescue their brothers.

IV. BRINGING THE TRUTH
TO THE COUNTRY

The flight of slaves did more than deal a direct blow at the structure of the slavocracy, and more than precipitate organized anti-slavery activity. It also put fresh vigor and determination into the hearts of the Abolitionists, for as William Still, the Negro director of the key Philadelphia branch of the Underground, wrote, "the pulse of the four millions of slaves and their desire for freedom" were brought home to them, dramatically and incessantly, by the steady flow of new arrivals.

And it brought slavery to the thresholds of the American people. Early in 1847 a Maryland fugitive arrived at Bronson Alcott's home in Concord, Massachusetts. Alcott's Journal for February 9 reads:

Our friend the fugitive, who has shared now a week's hospitality with us, sawing and piling my wood, feels this new taste of freedom yet unsafe here in New England, and so has left us for Canada. We supplied him with the means of journeying, and bade him a good god-speed to a freer land. . . . He is scarce thirty years of age, athletic, dextrous, sagacious, and self-relying. He has many of the elements of the hero. *His stay with us has given image and a name to the dire entity of slavery* and was an impressive lesson to my children, bringing before them the wrongs of the black man and his tale of woes. [Italics mine—*H.A.*]

Frequently, spectacular escapes of slaves, or attempts to rescue apprehended fugitives, or legal battles waged by anti-slavery groups to prevent the return of Negroes did for the nation as a whole what these individual visits did for families like the Alcotts. A few examples of cases that attracted great attention may be offered.

In the year 1842 a slave named Nelson Hackett escaped from Arkansas and made his way to Canada, a pilgrimage of some 1,100 miles. The governor of the state started extradition proceedings on the grounds of burglary, since of course Hackett did not own the clothes he wore. The governor-general of Canada returned Nelson Hackett, but he escaped again, and was again captured; a third time this redoubtable Negro fled from slavery and this time he was not retaken.

In 1843, seven slaves got into a small boat in Florida and sailed out to sea, their destination, freedom. For seven weeks they braved the ocean, were finally picked up by a British vessel, and reached the Bahamas, exhausted, famished, but free.

Two Virginia slaves, a man and wife, she almost white in appearance, escaped by traveling as master and slave, the woman disguised as a sickly young man, and the husband as "his" faithful attendant. Thus, in 1849, William and Ellen Craft appeared before the amazed eyes of America to tell their story; they told it also in Canada and in England.

Peculiar freight was hauled in 1848 from Richmond to Philadelphia (a twenty-six-hour trip in those days) by the Adams Express Company. For in a trunk three feet long, two feet wide, and less than three feet deep lay a man, Henry Brown, with biscuits and water. That trunk had been forwarded by a white man, a shoe dealer named Samuel A. Smith, to a Philadelphia agent of the Underground. Henry "Box" Brown arrived safely, and tremendous gatherings of people in many Northern cities came to hear him explain why he preferred a twenty-six-hour trip in a coffin to remaining contented and happy as a slave.

Not all of these stories end happily. Margaret Garner, her husband, and three children reached a Negro agent's house on the outskirts of Cincinnati, but their trail was picked up, and they were captured after a bitter fight. Mrs. Garner attempted to kill her children and herself, but succeeded only in killing a daughter. She said it was better that way, for the child would now never know what a woman suffers as a slave. She begged to be tried for murder for she "will go singing to the gallows rather than be returned to slavery"; but her wish was denied and the master regained his property.

The masters often had a difficult time trying to recover their fugitive slaves even if they caught up with them. Slaves who had themselves felt the lash were skeptical of mere moral suasion as a means of converting America, slaveholders included, to an anti-slavery viewpoint. They did not share the faith expressed in the public pronouncements of the Garrisonian Abolitionists concerning the efficacy of such an appeal. In the words of one of them, the Reverend J. W. Loguen:

I want you to set me down as a *Liberator* man. Whether you will call me so or not, I am with you in heart. I may not be in hands and head—for my hands will fight a slaveholder—which I suppose the *Liberator* and some of its good friends would not do. . . . I am a fugitive slave, and you know that we have strange notions about many things.

Rescue attempts, apparently spontaneous in origin, but soon resulting from planned organizational work, were frequent and often spectacular enough to capture the entire nation's attention. A very early example of this occurred in Massachusetts in 1793, immediately after the passage of the Fugitive Slave Act of that year. A Negro was seized by one claiming to be his master and proceedings were instituted under the terms of the act for his return to the South. Josiah Quincy, son of the revolutionary patriot of the same name, a twenty-one-year old attorney who had just received his degree, brought what legal lore he had to the assistance of the Negro. He was about to begin his argument before the honorable court when a group of Negroes intent upon action rather than argument entered the room. Mr. Quincy "heard a noise, and turning around he saw the constable lying on the floor, and a passage opening through the crowd, through which the fugitive was taking his departure without stopping to hear the opinion of the court."

Such events continued to recur and to attract attention even before the birth of a nationwide Abolitionist movement in the 1830's. Indeed, there is evidence to show that Negroes had actually formed some sort of machinery for this very purpose, for by 1826 newspapers carried items complaining about the difficulty of returning escaped slaves. This, it was explained, arose because news of such an attempt quickly spread and brought crowds of Negroes who always tried and often succeeded in making off with the captive.

In the generation prior to the Civil War not a year and scarcely a month passed without such an event. This aided in publicizing the Abolitionist movement and in activizing large groups of the population. A few examples will illustrate this:

A Baltimore slaveholder arrived in Boston in 1836 and directed a sheriff to arrest two Negroes who, he said, had fled from him. This was done, but in August of that year a large number of Negroes, mostly women, succeeded, over the rather inert opposition of the sheriff (who was Charles Sumner's father), in getting at the fugitives and safely spiriting them away.

Six years later another exciting case aroused the populace of the same city and had wide repercussions. A Virginia slave, Latimer, was arrested by state officers and was about to be returned when news of the occurrence spread. Mass meetings were held and when it was learned that the master would manumit Latimer for the sum of $400 the money was quickly raised, and the Negro became a free man. Latimer became active in subsequent agitational work, and his case was an important factor in bringing about in 1842 the passage by the Massachusetts legislature of a Personal Liberty Law which forbade state officials from taking part in the enforcement of the federal laws concerning rendition of fugitive slaves. During the next six years, five other Northern states passed similar legislation which greatly aggravated, in the minds of the slaveholders, the fugitive slave problem, and moved them to pass the drastic and infamous Act of 1850. This in turn was one of the precipitants of the crises that were characteristic of the next decade.

The Act of 1850 provided for the appointment of special Federal commissioners to aid in slave hunting and forced all United States marshals and deputies whom they might appoint to aid in the search. One needed but convince a commissioner of the Negro's identity—and in this process only the white person's testimony was acceptable —in order to have the Negro turned over to the claimant. All citizens were liable to a call to aid in the prosecution of the statute. The decision of the commissioner was final, and his fee was $5 if he discharged the Negro, and $10 if he decided he was indeed a fugitive slave!

The first case that arose from this act is indicative of how firm and united was the response of the Negro people to its challenge. On the day the law became effective a Miss Brown of Baltimore claimed a free Negro, James Hamlet, of New York City as her slave, convinced the commissioner of this, and had the man shipped off to her home before he was able to communicate with anyone. Soon, however, the facts were learned: 1,500 Negroes gathered at a church, subscribed a total of $500, and with this ransomed Hamlet.

Vigilance committees, made up of Negro and white, sprang up throughout the North. Their purpose was to block the arrest or bring about the rescue of fugitive slaves, thus making the raising of ransom money unnecessary. An action which took place in New Bedford, Massachusetts, was typical: "Between six and seven hundred colored citizens many of whom are fugitives are here and are determined to stand by one another and live or die together. The colored citizens abandoned their separate places of worship and assembled in a body at Liberty Hall," where they let the world in general, and slaveholders and their agents in particular, know that those who sought to enslave them would be faced with unity and militancy.

Thousands, Negro and white, were involved in subsequent rescue attempts, many successful, such as those of Shadrach in Boston, Jerry in Syracuse, Johnson in Chicago in 1851, and Glover in Racine, Wisconsin, in 1854. A slaveholder named Gorsuch experienced this unity and militancy one day in September, 1851, when he, together with professional man catchers and some United States deputy marshals, arrived in Sadsbury, Pennsylvania, seeking a fugitive slave who was being sheltered at the home of a free Negro named William Parker. The Philadelphia vigilance committee, headed by William Still, had advance notice of Gorsuch's mission and they responded at once by sending an agent, again a Negro, to warn the people at Sadsbury.

Gorsuch arrived, demanded the fugitive, and was refused. The Parker home was then attacked. Its owner sounded a horn and swarms of Negroes rushed to the scene, armed with clubs, axes, and a few guns. A battle ensued, the slave catchers were routed, several were wounded, and Gorsuch himself was killed. About thirty Negroes, among whom were Susan Clark, Eliza Brown, Harvey Scott, Miller Thompson, and William Parker, and two white friends, Castner Hanway and Elijah Lewis, were arrested and charged with treason and with levying war against the government of the United States. The defense was conducted by two outstanding lawyers, John M. Read and Thaddeus Stevens. These men conducted the defense eloquently. The sympathies of the people were very largely with the defendants, and every one of them was acquitted, a resounding victory for the antislavery cause.

At rare intervals in these cases the slaveholders, backed by the might of the Federal government, won, and the slaves were returned. But these were Pyrrhic victories, because the commotion and excitement attending the return of every slave meant that the question of slavery had been brought before the minds of tens of thousands of people.

Outstanding among these were the cases of Thomas

Sims in 1851 and Anthony Burns in 1854, both occurring in Boston.

Thomas Sims had fled from Georgia and was living in Boston. In the evening of April 3, 1851, he was arrested on the demand of his master. Tremendous agitation swept the city in the ensuing hours. Deputy marshals, police, and militia swarmed over the city, and huge chains were swung around the courthouse in which the commissioner was deciding Sim's fate. Only these precautions prevented the city's Negroes, aided by their white allies (including Thomas Wentworth Higginson and Theodore Parker), from forcibly rescuing the manacled human offering of appeasement.

The commissioner chose to earn $10 rather than $5 in this case, and Thomas Sims, heavily guarded, was sent back to Savannah and slavery. There he was severely whipped in public, jailed for two months, sold to a slave trader in Charleston, thence shipped to New Orleans and finally bought for work as a mason in Vicksburg. And, not very much later, when Grant's men were besieging Vicksburg in 1863, one of the many slaves who escaped to that army of liberation was Thomas Sims, who was dispatched to the North as a prize of war and as a returning hero.

Characteristic responses to this case were recorded by two individuals in almost the same words at the height of the excitement. Theodore Parker commented bitterly, "A few years ago they used to tell us, 'Slavery is an abtraction.' 'We at the North have nothing to do with it.'" And Bronson Alcott remarked, "The question 'What has the North to do with slavery?' is visibly answered."

The Anthony Burns case was an even greater sensation. This young man escaped from Richmond in February, 1854, and made his way to Boston. Agents of his master traced him and in May, 1854, his case came before the commissioner. Quite by chance, Richard H. Dana, who was in the courtroom at the moment, came to the defense of the Negro, and sent out the first public word of the affair.

The news spread like wildfire; spontaneous monster protest meetings took place, and militant Abolitionists led by the Negro, Lewis Hayden, and by Thomas Wentworth Higginson, attempted to crash the prison's bars and free Anthony Burns, but they failed. On June 2 a groaning, hissing, straining mass of humanity lined the streets of Boston and watched a lone, handcuffed man being led back to slavery. Twenty-two companies of state militia, four platoons of marines, a battalion of United States artillerymen, and the city's police force were used to ensure the performance of this shameful act, the cost of which, to the Federal government alone, came to $40,000.

Bronson Alcott's entry in his journal indicates clearly the effect of this upon a broad segment of public opinion, moving some of it to a demand for militant action:

Witness Burns's rendition today sadly, and ashamed of the Union, of New England, of Boston, almost of myself too. I must see to it that my part is done hereafter to give us a Boston, a mayor, a governor and a President—if indeed a single suffrage, or many, can mend matters essentially. So I shall vote as I have never done hitherto, for a municipal government and a state. Possibly a country may yet be rescued from slavery. ... Yet something besides voting must do it effectually.

That many vowed as did Alcott is demonstrated by the fact that every Massachusetts official who took part in returning Burns was retired from public life at the next election.

Sufficient funds were soon raised by public subscriptions to free Burns. He spent two years at Oberlin College and at the Fairmount Theological Seminary in Cincinnati, and then toured the country making anti-slavery speeches.

In his own words, these were illustrated by "a panorama, styled the Grand Moving Mirror—scenes of real life, startling and thrilling incidents, degradation and horrors of American slavery."

V. ORGANIZED ANTI-SLAVERY EFFORTS

This type of work on the part of Burns is indicative of the organized anti-slavery activities of the Negro people which began long before the 1850's and continued until the battle was won.

We have, hitherto, focused our attention, with the exception of the Underground Railroad, upon the unorganized, spontaneous phases of the anti-slavery struggle, and extraneous factors affecting its strength, rather than upon the movement itself as an organized, disciplined, cohesive force.

Cohesiveness, discipline, organization were vital if the Abolitionist cause was to succeed, for its purpose was of a profoundly revolutionary nature. Unless the effort is seen in this light its character is but dimly grasped, for the Abolitionists set themselves the task of subverting and destroying a fundamental vested interest whose roots were deep and whose branches were far spread.

It is true that success finally came only after the maturing of a new class, the industrial bourgeoisie, whose interests were opposed to those of its predecessor, but this success was not automatic, did not come of itself. It was produced by men and women, Negro and white, who had for decades been sowing the seed, talking, writing, petitioning, voting, and who finally piloted an aroused America through the maelstrom of a four-year Civil War. How much work had to be done before the nation willingly set itself the task of excising the cancer of slavery from its vitals; before a long-legged Westerner named Lincoln would agree that the operation should continue even though it go on "until all the wealth piled by the bondsman's 250 years of unrequited toil shall be sunk, and until every drop of blood drawn by the lash shall be paid by another drawn with the sword"!

The job was not for the faint-hearted. The slaveholders represented for the first half of the nineteenth century the most closely knit and most important single economic unit in the nation, their millions of bondsmen and millions of acres of land comprising an investment of billions of dollars. This economic might had its counterpart in political power giving its possessors dominance within the nation and predominance within the South. Listen to the words of James Hammond, a rich slaveholder and leading South Carolina politician. Commenting in 1845 on the bitterness of the words passing between the slaveholding and Abolitionist groups, he addressed the latter:

But if your course was wholly different—if you distilled nectar from your lips and discoursed sweetest music, could you reasonably indulge the hope of accomplishing your object by such means? Nay, supposing that we were all convinced, and thought of Slavery precisely as you do, at what era of "moral suasion" do you imagine you could prevail on us to give up a thousand millions of dollars in the value of our slaves, and a thousand millions of dollars more in the depreciation of our lands, in consequence of the want of laborers to cultivate them?

And the products wrung from these slaves and this land, the rice, sugar, cotton, tobacco, made up the blood and bones of the businesses of the merchant capitalists of the North; they, too, rested finally upon the broad black backs of the slaves, and so they allied themselves with the Negro's immediate exploiters. Thus it was that a partner in a large New York mercantile house summoned Samuel J. May, the Abolitionist, one day in 1835, and said:

Mr. May, we are not such great fools as not to know that slavery is a great evil and a great wrong. But it was consented to by the founders of the Republic. It was provided for in the Constitution of our Union. A great portion of the property of the Southerners is invested under its sanction; and the business of the North as well as of the South, has became adjusted to it. There are millions upon millions of dollars due from the Southerners to the merchants and mechanics of this city alone, the payment of which would be jeopardized by a rupture between the North and the South. We cannot afford, sir, to let you and your associates succeed in your endeavor to overthrow slavery. It is not a matter of principle with us. It is a matter of business necessity. We cannot afford to let you succeed. And I have called you out to let you know, and to let your fellow laborers know, that we do not mean to allow you to succeed. We mean, sir, to put you Abolitionists down—by fair means, if we can, by foul means, if we must.

And if all this were not enough, the slaveholders did not fail to appreciate, and to point out to their Northern class brothers, that the philosophy of Abolitionism—its equalitarianism, its progressivism, and, above all, its attack upon the sanctity of private property—represented an ultimate threat to the interests of all exploiters. As a Virginian wrote in reply to the questioning of the institution of slavery that flowered following the Nat Turner cataclysm:

This one thing we wish to be understood and remembered—that the Constitution of this state, has made Tom, Dick, and Harry, *property*—it has made Polly, Nancy, and Molly, *property;* and be that property an evil, a curse, or what not, we intend to hold it. Property, which is considered the most valuable by the owners of it, is a nice thing; and for the right thereto, to be called in question by an unphilosophical set of political mountebanks, under the influence of supernatural agency or deceit, is insufferable.

Somewhat later, John W. Underwood, a wealthy Georgian, warned that the "same torch" which, wielded by the Abolitionists, threatened to consume the fabric of the slave South would, one day, "also cause the northeastern horizon to coruscate with the flames of northern palaces." The essence of the matter was more fully put by a religious and educational leader of South Carolina, Dr. James H. Tornwell, in 1850:

The parties in this conflict are not merely Abolitionists and slaveholders—they are atheists, socialists, communists, red republicans, Jacobins on the one side, and the friends of order and regulated freedom on the other. In one word, the world is the battleground—Christianity and atheism the combatants; and the progress of humanity the stake.

Yes, the Abolitionists were attacking the lords of the lash who controlled the press and pulpit, who represented stability and respectability, and who manipulated the political apparatus. To conquer them required wisdom, level-headedness, energy, organization, and, above all, perfect courage, rooted in deep-seated overwhelming conviction that human slavery was bad, evil, rotten—a courage and a conviction that scorned compromise, detested opportunism, and gained strength from the enemy's resistance.

Where would this conviction reside if not in the hearts and minds of Negro Americans? Who would better know slavery than those whose backs bore its stripes, into whose eyes had been blazoned its indignities and abominations; who, while they spoke and wrote and agitated, were speaking and writing and agitating about that which, even while they labored, was oppressing their own people, often their own children, or their own parents?

VI. THE EIGHTEENTH CENTURY

From the era of the first American Revolution through the years of the second, Negroes were ever in the vanguard of the organized army attacking the slavocracy, seeking out and using to the uttermost whatever possibilities existed to advance the struggle.

Evidence of concerted Abolitionist activity on the part of the Negro people goes back at least to the 1760's when, in Massachusetts, they attempted to challenge the entire legal concept of slavery by bringing an action of trespass against their masters. The next decade was marked by a petition campaign, organized and carried on by Negroes, in which provincial and state governing bodies were urged to destroy slavery, on the ground, as one of the documents put it: "That the God of Nature gave them life and freedom, upon the terms of most perfect equality with other men; That freedom is an inherent right of the human species, not to be surrendered, but by consent, for the sake of social life." There are extant records of eight such petitions, some signed by "a Grate Number of Blackes," in Massachusetts and New Hampshire from 1773 to 1779. One of these, presented in 1775 by Negroes of Bristol and Worcester to the Committee of Correspondence of the latter county, led to the holding of a convention on June 14 of many citizens, which went on record as abhorring Negro slavery and pledging to work for its abolition.

This type of agitation was continued during the remaining years of the eighteenth century and, in addition, one may discern during the same period the beginnings of the Negro's contribution to the vast body of anti-slavery literature and the birth of Negro organizations for emancipation. Particularly to be noted are the petitions of Prince Hall, a Massachusetts Negro, Masonic official, and veteran of the Revolutionary War, and of Absalom Jones, the Pennsylvania religious leader.

The petition signed by Prince Hall alone was presented early in 1788 to the Massachusetts legislature and was aimed at getting that body to outlaw the slave trade. It attracted considerable attention, was the subject of correspondence between such figures as Jeremy Belknap and Ebenezer Hazard, and was printed in full in the Boston *Spy* of April 24, 1788. Other petitions, from white people, followed, and this type of pressure and publicity was influential in bringing about the passage that year of a state ban upon the trade.

The other petition was drawn up in 1799 and signed by "Absalom Jones and others, free men of color, of the city and county of Philadelphia," and presented on January 2, 1800, to the Congress of the United States by Representative Waln. This asked for a Federal anti-slave-trade law, the repeal of the Fugitive Slave Act of 1793, and "the adoption of such measures as shall in due course emancipate the whole of their brethren from their present situation." It provoked an exceedingly sharp and long debate, lasting two days, and was the means of focusing national attention upon the abomination. The petition was finally accepted and referred (and then buried), but only after the House had added the statement that the petitioners, by their boldness and audacity in asking Congress to abolish slavery, had earned the "disapprobation" of the members—and this by a vote of 85 to 1, Mr. Waln alone having the honor of casting a negative vote.

The pen was also wielded for the cause, even this early in the nation's history. One of the leading magazines in the country, the *American Museum,* published in Philadelphia by Mathew Carey, ran articles written by Negroes (one signed "Othello," the other "A Free Negro") in 1788 and 1789, denouncing slavery and demanding the realization in practice of the Declaration of Independence. The latter article was especially effective, stressing the fact that while white revolutionists were hailed as heroes and martyrs, Negroes who essayed the same task were greeted with derision and treated like depraved criminals. "Do rights of nature cease to be such when a Negro is to enjoy them?" this writer demanded. "Or does patriotism in the heart of an African rankle into treason?"

Others, including Prince Hall, Benjamin Banneker, Absalom Jones, and Richard Allen, published pamphlets in the 1790's in which every essential argument of the Abolitionist movement was enunciated and developed. These works denied the inferiority of the Negro, gave the lie to assertions that the slaves were happy and docile, and warned that the longer the evil continued, the more costly and catastrophic would be its destruction.

The beginnings of Negro organization likewise go back to these years, and no matter what the ostensible purposes of these groups were—religious, philanthropic, or literary —the very act on the part of these oppressed people of joining together was itself revolutionary, and they all, sooner or later, became part and parcel of the entire anti-slavery crusade. In the spring of 1787 Philadelphia Negroes, including Richard Allen, Absalom Jones, William White, Mark Stevenson, William Gray, and others, formed a Free African Society whose original stated purpose was largely convivial, but which by 1790 devoted itself to anti-slavery agitation, the prevention of Negro kidnaping, and co-operation with other emancipationist groups, such as state manumission societies and Quakers. Shortly afterward Henry Stewart, a member of this society, moved to Newport, Rhode Island, and established a similar association there. Another such group was formed in New York City in 1795, and within three years still another African Society sprang up in Boston. The interests of the latter society are sufficiently indicated by the fact that it published, in 1808, a pamphlet entitled, *The Sons of Africa: An Essay on Freedom with Observations on the Origin of Slavery.*

VII. EARLY NINETEENTH CENTURY

The first generation of the nineteenth century witnessed a significant expansion in the anti-slavery activities of the Negro people which did much to prepare the ground for the tilling and harvesting that was to come from 1830 to the Civil War. Among the individuals who stand out during this formative period was Peter Williams, Jr., a minister in New York City, whose efforts to arouse his countrymen to the iniquities of slavery attracted attention as early as 1806. His work in this field continued for thirty years and led to his appointment in 1834 to the Board of Managers of the American Anti-Slavery Society. Events such as large-scale meetings of Negroes occurred in 1807 and 1808 in various Northern cities, notably Philadelphia and New York, celebrating the passage, and the coming into force, of the Federal anti-slave-trade law and contributing toward the publicizing of the cause of freedom.

A few years later another Negro whose career was to continue on into the 'thirties, James Forten of Philadelphia, made himself felt on behalf of his people's liberation. He gained notice in 1813 by his vigorous denunciation of projected Jim Crow regulations in Pennsylvania and in 1817, together with Russell Parrott, was important in bringing together three thousand Philadelphia Negroes. These people went on record as being decidedly opposed to the purposes of the recently launched American Colonization Society and as determined to win justice for themselves and their enslaved brethren here in their native land, rather than to seek a doubtful refuge elsewhere and so withdrawing from the struggle for the slaves' emancipation. In the words of the assembled thousands:

Let not a purpose be assisted which will stay the cause of the entire abolition of slavery in the United States, and which may defeat it altogether; which proffers to those who do not ask for them *benefits*, but which they consider *injuries*, and which must insure to the multitudes, whose prayers can only reach through us, *misery, sufferings, and perpetual slavery*.

This early meeting and expression of opinion are indicative of the viewpoint of the Negro people. Their wellnigh unanimous opposition was of the utmost importance in crippling the colonization movement (which received support and money from numerous wealthy individuals and even state legislatures, such as those of Maryland and Virginia), and in winning William Lloyd Garrison away from the snare and toward his unequivocal demand for immediate abolition of slavery.

The next decade was marked by worldwide development of progressivism, the most striking manifestation of which in the United States was the triumph of Jacksonianism and the lusty beginnings of a politically conscious labor movement. The growth of anti-slavery feeling was notable, particularly in Great Britain, and keen observers, such as Thomas Jefferson and John Quincy Adams, prophesied as early as 1820 the speedy crystallization of the struggle between the free and the slave systems.

Negroes, ever in the forefront of those struggling against slavery, anticipated and did vital spade work for the flowering of the Abolitionist movement, which came in the 'thirties. Of importance in the immediately preceding years were the Reverend Nathaniel Paul of the African Baptist Society in Albany, New York, whose radical speeches began to attract attention in 1827, the Reverend John Gloucester of Philadelphia, and William Whipper of the same city. The latter was influential in starting a Reading Room Society in Philadelphia in 1828, the broad purpose of which was the general education of its Negro members and, specifically, the development of anti-slavery sentiment. Similar groups sprang up elsewhere (sometimes demonstrating their emancipation motive in their names, such as the New York African Clarkson Society, 1829). Thus it was that by the time the national anti-slavery groups were formed early in the 'thirties, there already existed about fifty such Negro organizations spread throughout the country and eager to assist and join forces with the newcomers.

The cause had developed sufficiently among the Negro people for them to be able to create and to support a weekly organ devoted to its enhancement. On March 16, 1827, *Freedom's Journal* was published in New York City under the editorship of Samuel E. Cornish and John Russwurm. The journal had agents throughout New England, New York, Pennsylvania, Maryland, the District of Columbia, and even in Virginia and North Carolina, as well as in Haiti, Canada, and England.

One of the Boston agents of *Freedom's Journal* was David Walker, a key figure in the history of the Abolitionist movement. He had been born free in North Carolina on September 28, 1785, but the enslavement of his fellow men disgusted and enraged him and he decided he had to "leave this part of the country." He went to Boston, where he earned his bread by dealing in old clothes. Here he became active in anti-slavery work, spoke before the Colored Association of that city in December, 1828, and occasionally contributed to, as well as distributed, *Freedom's Journal.*

In September, 1829, he published his *Appeal,* and from then, until his mysterious death sometime in 1830,* he supervised the distribution and reprinting of this work, which during the last year of his life went into its third edition. And David Walker, back in 1829, went as far as, and in some respects further than, Abolitionist literature in general was to go for another twenty years. He used the Declaration of Independence with telling effect, flinging its immortal words into the teeth of those who upheld slavery. He denounced the Colonizationists and affirmed the Negro's right to the title of American. He excoriated the traitors among his own people, finding it difficult to find words damning enough with which to express his contempt for them. He waxed sarcastic, and exuded bitterness as he contemplated the prevailing hypocrisy, when everyone *talked* about liberty and equality, while millions of human beings were treated worse than brutes. Rebel, he told the slaves, rebel and when "you commence make sure work—do not trifle, for they will not trifle with you—they want us for their slaves and think nothing of murdering us in order to subject us to that wretched condition—therefore, if there is an *attempt* made by us, kill or be killed."

At only one point did David Walker leave the immediate and the practical, and he did this in order to utter this prophecy:

. . . for although the destruction of the oppressors God may not effect by the oppressed, yet the Lord our God will bring

---

* "A colored Bostonian" reported in the *Liberator,* Jan. 22, 1831, that it was believed Walker had been murdered. A rumor was current that some person or persons in the South had offered $3,000 reward to the individual who would kill him.

146

other destructions upon them—for not infrequently will he cause them to rise up one against another, to be split and divided, and to oppress each other, and sometimes to open hostilities with sword in hand.

Walker's *Appeal* was sent by him, through Negro and white sympathizers, into the South and caused great excitement when discovered in Georgia, Louisiana, and North Carolina.

In 1829 there appeared two other pamphlets from the pens of Negroes. One, called *The Ethiopian Manifesto,* was written by Robert Alexander Young of New York City. Its style is peculiar and mystical, its language biblical, but its message—damning the system of slavery—is clear. A note of militancy appears in the prophesying of the coming of a Negro messiah who shall be invincible and who shall forcibly achieve the liberation of his people. The other, printed in Raleigh (and reissued in Philadelphia in 1837) was the product of a North Carolina slave, George Moses Horton, and consisted of several poems, the essence of which was clearly expressed in the title, *The Hope of Liberty.*

The same year also marks the appearance of the second Negro newspaper, *The Rights of All,* which Samuel E. Cornish brought out in New York shortly after Russwurm's renegacy had forced the *Freedom's Journal* to suspend publication. *The Rights of All* was a radical paper of the highest integrity and quality, and while it lasted but a short time it led the way for a host of other Negro newspapers that shortly followed and that were devoted to, and valued adjuncts of, the Abolitionist movement.

Another major event that antedated the appearance of the *Liberator,* and was a forerunner of similar events which were to play an important part during the years of the pre-Civil War generation, was the assembling of the first national Negro Convention in Philadelphia in September, 1830. This convention denounced the American Colonization Society, called for the slaves' liberation, advocated improved educational and industrial opportunities for Negroes, and formed the American Society for Free Persons of Color to protect and assist such people and to secure a refuge for escaped slaves in Canada. In December of the same year a meeting of several hundred Negroes took place in Richard Allen's Philadelphia church, presided over by Ignatius Beek. A Free Produce Society was formed here with a membership of about two hundred and thirty people pledged to abstain from the use of slave-produced commodities, a boycott movement which had played and which continued to play a fairly large part in the general anti-slavery struggle, both in the United States and in Europe.

VIII. THE PRE-CIVIL WAR GENERATION

These independent efforts of the Negro people continued during the years when large numbers of white people entered into the battle. Thus there existed, in addition to the literary and social organizations, all-Negro Abolitionist societies in many parts of the country. Some, like the Massachusetts General Colored Association, established in 1832 under the leadership of Thomas Dalton and William C. Nell, preceded the formation of the American Anti-Slavery Society. Many such organized bodies existed throughout the nation in cities like New York, Philadelphia, Boston, Newark; Albany, Rochester and Geneva, New York; Middletown, Connecticut; Nantucket,

Massachusetts; Lexington, Ohio; and Lexington, Kentucky.

There is also evidence of the existence of Negro societies which had as their objective even more dangerous tasks than the sheltering of fugitives and the spreading of the literature and ideas of Abolitionism. These were dedicated to the aim of overthrowing slavery by every and any possible way, not excepting militant action, and to organizing the rescue of Negroes from slavery by entering the South and helping them escape. The dangerous character of the work of these groups and their illegality demanded secrecy, so that information concerning them is scarce. However, there is information that points to the fact that in 1844, the Reverend Moses Dickson of Cincinnati, together with eleven other Negroes, founded an "Order of Twelve of the Knights and Daughters of Tabor," which had the aims indicated above. In 1846 Dickson started another secret association, the Knights of Liberty, with headquarters in St. Louis. This association aided hundreds of slaves to escape.

In addition to these permanent organizations, conventions of Negroes called to combat slavery, assist Abolitionist societies and publications, fight Jim Crowism and strive for the betterment of conditions for free Negroes, were regular features of America's ante-bellum years. National conventions were held annually from 1830 on, steadily growing in the number of delegates and the areas represented, the chief meeting places being New York and Philadelphia. State conventions also assembled frequently in various parts of the country, while from time to time when such special issues as colonization, battles against Jim Crowism, or aid to progressive forces, became acute, spontaneous, enthusiastic and well-attended meetings were held.

Characteristic examples may be presented. The fifth

annual convention of Negroes of New York state was held September 18-20, 1844, in Schenectady. This was attended by over eighty delegates from eighteen cities and towns in the state, including Albany, Amsterdam, Ballston, Brooklyn, Constantia, Peterstown, Rochester, Syracuse, Troy, and Waterford. Men like the Reverend Henry Highland Garnet, Patrick H. Reason, Stephen Myers, and Dr. James McCune Smith were present. Resolutions demanding absolute equality, immediate emancipation, and total abstinence from slave-produced goods were adopted.

Reference has already been made to anti-colonization meetings held by Negroes soon after the launching of that obnoxious scheme. Similar affairs occurred whenever this movement showed signs of regaining vigor. This was particularly true in 1831 when, as a result of the marked increase of restlessness among the slaves, the master class turned to colonization with heightened ardor.

Typical was the meeting held in African Hall on Nassau Street in Brooklyn, New York, in May, 1831, where the Negroes affirmed, "that we are *men,* that we are *brethren,* that we are *countrymen* and *fellow citizens"* and found it strange indeed that the eminent gentlemen of the Colonization Society "can promise to honor and respect us in Africa, when they are using every effort to exclude us from all rights and privileges at home."

Every Negro meeting and convention attacked chauvinism, but some were wholly devoted to the subject or to some specific manifestation of it. Thus, legal discriminations against the suffrage of New York Negroes moved them to hold repeated meetings in the 1830's with men like Charles L. Reason and Thomas L. Jennings particularly prominent in protesting the disability. A petition campaign was organized, agents tramped through the country and succeeded in getting thousands of signatures, though their efforts were not crowned with success for many years. Similarly, in the 'forties, mass meetings and conventions were organized by Negroes in Ohio in order to secure the repeal of the Black Codes, with John M. Langston, George Carey, David Jenkins, and Denis Hill leading the battle. This was successful, so that in 1849 Ohio's discriminatory legislation was repealed.

Others prominent in this never-ending struggle against Jim-Crowism in many different parts of the country were Frederick Douglass, Sojourner Truth, Robert Purvis, David Ruggles, Archie P. Webb, Charles L. Remond, Theodore S. Wright, and William C. Nell, the tactics used varying from law suits and petition campaigns to mass demonstrations and physical resistance.

Encouragement and assistance for progressive forces were often the main purposes of Negro meetings. Thus Philadelphia Negroes, led by Frederick Hinton, William Whipper, Robert Purvis, James Forten, and Junius C. Morell, met on March 1, 1831, only two months after the launching of the *Liberator*, pledged their support to it, and contributed to its maintenance. Such gatherings were common in various cities throughout the paper's life.

A final and very important contribution made independently by the Negro people to the Abolitionist movement came through their own publications, which included newspapers, magazines, pamphlets, and books. Records exist of well over a score of weekly newspapers owned, edited, and published by Negroes and very largely devoted to the anti-slavery effort. New York City was the favorite locale of these organs, but they carried on in several other areas, Philadelphia, Pittsburgh, Albany, Troy, Rochester, Syracuse, Cincinnati, Cleveland, Baltimore, and San Francisco. Beginning in 1841, there also existed magazines, both monthly and quarterly, produced by Negroes, in which more substantial contributions to the same movement appeared.

Of the anti-slavery books produced by Negroes (largely autobiographical) one can select for notice here only a few of those which were most influential in creating and molding public opinion, for an attempt at compiling a list of all the books that flooded the bookstores would require many pages. Restricting ourselves to a dozen autobiographical works that were not equaled by any other single piece of writing so far as depicting the essence of the institution of slavery is concerned, we may note the narratives of Charles Ball, Henry Bibb, William Wells Brown (this former slave also produced, prior to the Civil War, a travel book, a collection of anti-slavery songs, a novel, and a play); Lewis and Milton Clarke, Josiah Henson (his work so moved a woman named Harriet Beecher Stowe that in 1850 she visited and conversed with him in Boston—an important force behind the production, in 1852, of her epoch-making *Uncle Tom's Cabin);* Jeremiah W. Loguen, Solomon Northrup, James W. C. Pennington (the life of this fugitive slave and militant Abolitionist, who earned the degree of Doctor of Divinity from Heidelberg University sold out its first edition of six thousand copies within the year); Austin Steward, Sojourner Truth, Samuel R. Ward, and, in a class by itself in this literature, the forthright and moving autobiography of Frederick Douglass, first published in Boston in 1845. This classic was bought by eleven thousand people within the United States by the end of 1847; in the same brief period it went through nine editions in Great Britain, was translated into French and German, and throughout the struggle was one of the most widely read works of all ante-bellum writings.

Important works of a historical and sociological nature aiding the cause of Abolitionism were also produced by Negroes. Especially noteworthy were two sharp and biting pamphlets published in New York in 1834 and 1838 by

David Ruggles; a pioneer historical work by James W. C. Pennington; an excellent brief work on Toussaint L'Ouverture by Dr. James McCune Smith; a full-length and still very useful study of the Negro's role in American history by William C. Nell; and a detailed socio-economic monograph by Martin R. Delany. Near the end of the ante-bellum era an "Afric-American Printing Company" was established in New Haven, this being "an association for the publication of Negro literature," which has to its credit the issuance of at least one good short historical work.*

IX. UNITED STRUGGLES

Negroes did not, of course, restrict themselves to independent work, but struggled side by side with white people in the common effort. Thus, for example, the production and sustenance of the chief organ of the Abolitionist movement, the *Liberator,* published in Boston from 1831 to 1865 by William Lloyd Garrison, were made possible by the encouragement and aid of Negroes. From 1830 on, they wrote many letters to Garrison, giving not only moral stimulation, but also that kind of stimulation without which any publication perishes—money and subscriptions. Indeed, in the earliest and most trying years the number of Negro subscribers far outweighed that of white, so that in 1831 out of 450 subscribers, fully 400 were Negroes, and in 1834 "of the whole number of subscribers [2,300] to the *Liberator,* only about one-fourth are white."

* James T. Holly, *A Vindication of the Capacity of the Negro Race for Self-Government,* New Haven, 1857.

Contributions by Negroes to that paper and other Abolitionist publications were exceedingly common. The *Liberator* for February 12, 1831, furnishes an example. About a third of the paper's space is taken up by articles by two Philadelphia Negroes, a call to an anti-colonization mass meeting of Negroes in Boston, signed by James G. Barbadoes, Robert Roberts, Coffin Pitts, James T. Hilton, and Thomas Cole, and an account of a similar meeting recently held in New York under the leadership of Samuel Ennals and Philip Bell. This is fairly typical of the entire thirty-five volumes of the paper. Again, in the first issue of a popular annual called *Autographs for Freedom* one finds a biographical sketch of a Scottish Abolitionist, John Murray, by James McCune Smith, and a sixty-seven page history of the slave rebellion aboard the domestic slave trader *Creole*, by Frederick Douglass. And in the second issue of this work there are five articles on every phase of the movement by the Negro leaders, Charles L. Reason, John M. Langston, William W. Brown, James M. Smith, and Frederick Douglass, and two poems by Charles Reason and George B. Vashon.

Organizational work shows the same characteristics of joint participation. Three of the original signers of the declaration of the National Anti-Slavery Convention, held in Philadelphia in December, 1833, at which the American Anti-Slavery Society was formed, were Negroes: James G. Barbadoes, Robert Purvis, and James McCrummell; the committee which drew up this document included John G. Whittier, Samuel J. May, and William L. Garrison, who performed their task at the home of Frederick A. Hinton, a Philadelphia Negro. It is also an arresting fact that the first presiding officer of the Philadelphia Female Anti-Slavery Society was a Negro and a man, James McCrummell, a dentist. None of the ladies forming that organization felt competent to preside at a public meeting, and the only man they could find courageous enough to associate himself with two such slandered causes as Abolition and the active participation of women in public affairs was Dr. McCrummell.

Four of the original members of the Board of Managers of the American Anti-Slavery Society were Negroes: Peter Williams, Samuel E. Cornish, Theodore S. Wright, and Christopher Rush; the last three were members of its Executive Committee. In the later, more politically minded American and Foreign Anti-Slavery Society five Negroes were members of the Executive Committee: Samuel E. Cornish, Christopher Rush, George Whipple, Charles B. Ray, and James W. C. Pennington. In the organizational setup of the Abolitionist movement, Vigilance Committees on a local and state basis were key bodies since they protected fugitive slaves, aided free Negroes, and organized mass demonstrations. The directors of these committees in the most important centers, New York and Philadelphia, were both Negroes, Theodore S. Wright and William Still, respectively, while the corresponding secretary of the New York State Vigilance Committee was Charles B. Ray. Finally it is noteworthy that in 1847 Frederick Douglass was appointed president of the New England Anti-Slavery Society.

The record of the proceedings of any one of these Abolitionist organizations is studded with accounts of, or contributions by, Negroes. To take a few random examples: The 1849 meeting of the American and Foreign Anti-Slavery Society, held in New York City, was opened with an invocation by the Reverend Samuel R. Ward, a featured speaker was Henry Bibb, recently fled from Kentucky, and the entertainment was furnished by the four Luca boys, Negro youngsters, who sang an anti-slavery song called *Car of Emancipation*.

Again, at the 1853 meeting of the American Anti-

Slavery Society, held in Philadelphia, the audience heard a Negro gentleman of New Bedford, Massachusetts, the Reverend John J. Kelley, denounce slavery "with great earnestness" using "the plainest and most uncompromising language," and was then privileged to listen while Sojourner Truth sang "a plaintive song, touching the wrongs of the slave" and followed this with a speech, in her inimitably colorful manner, concerning "the wrong slavery had done to herself and others." And as an invigorating surprise a Negro lady, introduced as Mrs. Williams, said a few words. She lived in Wilmington, Delaware, and, though free herself, had seen slavery at first hand. She had heard and read of the terrible Abolitionists, inciters of violence, knaves, fools, fanatics, and decided to see these monsters for herself. Well, she had been sitting and listening, and she knew the Lord would bless them, for they were good and righteous folk. That is what she thought, and she did not care who knew it. Keep up the good fight, she said—and with this Mrs. Williams passes from history's pages.

Another rank-and-filer, whose very name is unknown, arranged an anti-slavery meeting all his own in the city of New York in 1833. In October, at Clinton Hall, the New York City Anti-Slavery Society was formed. The members of this meeting just managed to get out of the hall before a newspaper- and Tammany-incited pro-slavery mob arrived intent upon rooting out this subversive element. Frustrated by the emptiness of the hall, the mob pounced upon a passing Negro, constituted itself a mock Abolitionist meeting, placed the man on the platform, and demanded a speech. They got one, or as much of one as they would permit.

I am called upon to make a speech—said this unknown hero—You doubtless know that I am a poor, ignorant man, not accustomed to make speeches. But I have heard of the Declaration of Independence, and have read the Bible. The Declaration says all men are created equal, and the Bible says God has made us all of one blood. I think, therefore, we are entitled to good treatment, that it is wrong to hold men in slavery, and that—

but here shouts and blows stopped him. Yet, they had had their speech, had they not?

But thus far we have only *touched* upon the most vital part of the story. For the fate of the Abolitionist movement rested essentially on the backs of those who followed the sublime profession of agitators of the people, those who personified the heart and the conscience of the masses, those who, in the words of one of them, Sojourner Truth, served as fleas, mosquitoes, biting and stinging away at the vast giant of America—and Canada and Europe—until it was aroused to its obligation and duty and interest, and acted accordingly.

Contemporaries were keenly aware of the significance of these itinerant Negro arousers and probers. Back in 1839 a paper had aptly remarked of them:

They have men enough in action now to maintain the anti-slavery enterprise and to win their liberty and that of their enslaved brethren—if every white Abolitionist were drawn from the field: McCune Smith, and Cornish, and Wright, and Ray, and a host of others—not to mention our eloquent brother, Remond of Maine, and Brother Lewis who is stay and staff of field anti-slavery in New Hampshire.

William Lloyd Garrison gave similar testimony: "Who are among our ablest speakers? Who are the best qualified to address the public mind on the subject of slavery? Your fugitive slaves—your Douglasses, Browns and Bibbs —who are astonishing all with the cogency of their words and the power of their reasoning."

This cogency, and power, and eloquence were present because the speakers talked about that which they knew, that which they had seen and felt, that which affected them more directly and more forcefully than it did anyone else. And the very facts of their appearance, their bearing, courage, and intelligence were devastating anti-slavery forces.

They scoured the nation, visiting every state north of the Mason-Dixon Line, searching out every nook and cranny, with the incessant cry—Let my people go! The list of these valiant fighters for freedom includes all those who have already been mentioned and many others—like William Jones, Frances E. W. Harper, Henry Foster, Lunsford Lane, Charles Gardner, Andrew Harris, Abraham D. Shadd, David Nickens, and James Bradley.

Had none of these people existed but one, his existence and participation in the Abolitionist movement would justify the assertion that the Negro's role therein was decisive. That man is Frederick Douglass who, from his first public anti-slavery speech in 1841 to his organizing and recruiting activities during the war against the slavocracy, was *the* voice of America's millions of slaves. He, in the words of a white Abolitionist, Robert Raymond, was what fighters in that movement had been praying for: one who had known slavery and was eloquent, impressive, energetic, and fearless. There he stood, a magnificent figure of a man, impregnable, incorruptible, bearing slavery's scars upon his back, suffering, as he spoke, the anguish of knowing that a brother and four sisters were yet slaves. Those who once saw and heard Frederick Douglass never forgot him.

To Elizabeth Cady Stanton he appeared "like an African prince, conscious of his dignity and power, grand in his physical proportions, majestic in his wrath, as with keen wit, satire, and indignation he portrayed the bitterness of slavery, the humiliation of subjection to those who in all human virtues and capacities were inferior to himself." Wendell Phillips could only say, "He is one of our ablest men.'" A tailor in Bristol, England, after hearing him said he had never been so moved in his life and found it difficult to believe that such a man had been a slave only a few years before.

When Douglass met the despicable taunts about the inhumanity of the Negro, uttered by the Tammany ward-heeler, Police Captain Rynders, by facing him and demanding, "Am I a man?" the effect was nothing short of stupendous.

Douglass and his co-workers did not confine themselves to the United States. Negro fugitives in Canada formed the Windsor Anti-Slavery Society. The additional influx of Negroes after the Fugitive Slave Act of 1850 led to the formation in Toronto the next year of the Anti-Slavery Society of Canada under the leadership of Jeremiah W. Loguen and Samuel R. Ward. The importance of this work is graphically demonstrated by the fact that forty thousand Canadians enlisted in the Union Army during the Civil War.

England, Scotland, and Ireland were often visited by Negro Abolitionists, like Nathaniel Paul. Ellen and William Craft, Samuel R. Ward, Sarah P. Remond, Alexander Crummell, William Wells Brown, James W. C. Pennington, Henry Highland Garnet, Frederick Douglass, and Charles L. Redmond. After eighteen months' work Charles L. Remond returned in 1841 with an anti-slavery petition signed by sixty thousand men and women of Ireland, headed by Daniel O'Connell. The work was carried into France by William Wells Brown, while in 1850 Henry H. Garnet and James W. C. Pennington helped set up an anti-slavery society in Frankfort, Germany.

The facts relating to the part played by the Negro

people in the last acts of the drama of slavery's abolition, from John Brown's opening scene to the finale produced by Lincoln's army, have been developed elsewhere. Both scenes were made possible only through the Negro's participation. It was he who, in the words of Abraham Lincoln, when the final test came, "with silent tongue, and clenched teeth, and steady eye, and well-poised bayonet ...helped mankind on to this great consummation."

The history of the American Negro is filled with deeds of unsurpassed heroism and titanic efforts to realize his aspirations, and the aspirations of all other men, for equality and freedom. This is true from 1526, the year of the first slave rebellion in present-day South Carolina, to the efforts, more than three hundred years later, of the two hundred thousand men who shouldered muskets in Lincoln's Army of Liberation, and the thirty-six thousand among them who died in that Army's battles.

Of major importance in that history is the narrative of the prime role of the Negro people in carrying forward the Abolitionist movement. This brief sketch of their part in that epic crusade can close with no more fitting words than those uttered by a Negro minister, the Reverend Alexander Crummell, one of the combatants:

Let our posterity know that we their ancestors, uncultured and unlearned, amid all trials and temptations, were men of integrity; recognized with gratefulness their truest friends dishonoured and in peril; were enabled to resist the seductions of ease and the intimidations of power; were true to themselves, the age in which they lived, their abject race, and the cause of man; shrunk not from trial, nor from suffering:—but conscious of Responsibility and impelled by Duty, gave themselves up to the vindication of the high hopes, and the lofty aims of true Humanity!

THE NEGRO IN THE CIVIL WAR

I. INTRODUCTION

The time-worn myth that life in the old South was heavenly and that the slaves enjoyed an idyllic existence is repeated to this day. Hear, for example, an eminent professor, R. S. Cotterill, writing in the year 1936:

From the physical side his working hours were long but not strenuous; from the psychological side, since he had never known freedom, he looked upon slavery not as a degradation but as a routine. He took no thought of the future nor needed to. In sickness and in health, in his childhood and his old age he was assured of an income proportioned to his necessities and not to his productiveness.

This legend not only assures us of the slaves' contentment but it does something more. It tells us that the people who were enslaved—the Negro people—were, in any case, fit only to be slaves. We are assured that the Negro was, to quote a "standard historian," James Schouler, possessed of "innate patience, docility and child-like simplicity"; he was "an imitator and non-moralist, he learned deceit and libertinism with facility...his mind was not analytical" and he was "easily intimidated, incapable of deep plots." In plain English, says Schouler, the Negro was "sensuous, stupid, brutish, obedient."

From these two falsehoods—that slavery was delightful and that, in any case, the Negro was suited only for slavery —arises a third falsehood: that the American Negro rarely rebelled against his enslavement. To quote a work published in 1937, the Negro slave was "quite complacent." And from these same distortions come the erroneous gen-

163

eralizations regarding the Negro's behavior during the Civil War. Historians, if at all mentioning the Negro in their accounts of the war, describe him as an "element of strength" to the Confederacy, as "patiently submissive" (Rhodes, Phillips), as having "supported unanimously" the slavocracy (Cotterill).

But the facts contradict these fables. For two hundred years the American Negro people waged a persistent struggle against the diabolical system of chattel slavery, which was devised and continued for their super-exploitation. For sheer courage and ingenuity this conflict has never been surpassed in all the vast history of man's revolutionary struggles. In this desperate battle the Negroes carried on agitational and propagandistic work; they committed sabotage, they mutilated and killed themselves and their children rather than submit; they fled wherever there was a promise of freedom; they poisoned their masters, set fire to plantations, assassinated their oppressors; they conspired and rebelled, they waged guerrilla warfare, they gave up their lives fighting for the freedom of their people. And they eagerly grasped the opportunity offered by the Civil War to accentuate their struggles.

It is important to observe that at no period were these rebellious activities more widespread, and of deeper political significance (very often involving poor whites and even, at times, calling for a redistribution of the land, work animals and tools, as well as the end of slavery) than during the ten years immediately preceding the outbreak of the Civil War. It is beyond the scope of this brief study to recount the numerous plots and revolts which occurred. However, as an example, let us mention the events of this nature which took place in 1860, the last year before the slaveholders' rebellion.

Early in July fires swept over and devastated many cities and counties in northern Texas. Slaves were immediately

164

suspected and arrested. They were beaten, tortured and executed by the scores. *White men were invariably reported as being implicated,* and there were frequent notices of their being beaten and executed together with the slaves. Listing the counties in which plots were reported, cities burned and rebels executed will give an idea of the extensive character of the trouble and help explain the abject terror it aroused: Anderson, Austin, Dallas, Denton, Ellis, Grimes, Hempstead, Lamar, Milam, Montgomery, Rusk, Tarrant, Walker and Wood. The reign of terror in Texas lasted for about eight weeks.

Before it was over, reports of disaffection came from other areas. In August a conspiracy among the slaves, again with white accomplices, said to have been inspired by a nearby band of outlawed runaway slaves, was uncovered and crushed in Talladega county, Alabama. About one hundred miles south, in Pine Level, Montgomery county, of the same state, in that same month, the arrest of a white harness-maker was reported for "holding improper conversation with slaves." Within five months serious trouble was reported from that region.

Meanwhile, still in August, plots were uncovered in Whitfield, Cobb and Floyd counties in northwest Georgia. Said the Columbus, Georgia, *Sun* of August 29: "By a private letter from Upper Georgia, we learn that an insurrectionary plot has been discovered among the Negroes in the vicinity of Dalton and Marietta and great excitement was occasioned by it, and still prevails." The slaves had intended to burn Dalton, capture a train and crash on into Marietta some seventy miles away. Thirty-six of the slave leaders were imprisoned and the entire area took on a war-like aspect. Again it was felt that "white men instigated the plot," but, since Negro testimony was not acceptable against a white man, the proof against them was here felt to be insufficient for convictions. Another Georgia paper, the Augusta *Dispatch*, dated the same month, admitted: "We dislike to allude to the evidences of the insurrectionary tendency of things"; nevertheless it did deign to mention barely the recent discovery of a plot among the slaves of Floyd county, about forty miles northwest of Marietta.

In September a slave girl betrayed a conspiracy in Winston county, Mississippi. Approximately thirty-five slaves were arrested, and again it was discovered that whites were involved. At least one slave was hanged, as well as one white man, described as "an ambrotypist [photographer] named G. Harrington."

Late in October a plot, first formed in July, was disclosed among the slaves of Norfolk and Princess Anne counties, Virginia, and Currituck county, North Carolina. Jack and Denson, slaves of a Mr. David Corprew of Princess Anne, were among the leaders. Others were named Leicester, Daniel, Andrew, Jonas and William. These men planned to start the fight for freedom with their spades and axes and grubbing hoes. It was understood, according to a slave witness, that "white folks were to come in there to help us," but in no way could the rebels be influenced to name their white allies. Banishment, that is, sale and transportation out of the state, was the punishment for the slave leaders.

In November, plots were discovered in Crawford and Habersham counties, Georgia. In both places whites were involved. In Crawford a white man, described as a Northern tinsmith, was executed, while the white implicated in Habersham was given five hours to leave. How many slaves were involved is not clear. No executions among them were reported. According to the Southern papers the rebels were merely "severely whipped."

December found the trouble back again in the heart of Alabama, in Pine Level, Autaugaville, Prattville and

Hayneville. A resident of the region declared it involved "many hundred Negroes" and that "the instigators of the insurrection were found to be the low-down, or poor, whites of the country." It was discovered that the plot called for the redistribution of "the land, mules and money." Said another source, the Montgomery, Alabama, *Advertiser* of December 13:

We have found out a deep laid plot among the Negroes of our neighborhood, and from what we can find out from our Negroes, it is general all over the country.... We hear some startling facts. They have gone far enough in the plot to divide out our estates, mules, lands and household furniture.

The crop of martyrs in this particular plot numbered at least twenty-five Negroes and four whites. The names of but two of the whites are known, Rollo and Williamson.

It should be borne in mind that the preceding paragraphs summarize but one year in a decade of rebellious ferment, and but one of its manifestations.

The rulers of the South were keenly aware of this rebellious activity and seriously debated as to whether secession would aid in controlling the slaves and the poor whites, or whether secession would mean abolition. The slaveholders' decision—civil war—will be better understood when it is remembered that they had become desperate not only because they had seen their external, or national power almost completely overthrown by an emerging industrial, free-labor society, but also because they were seeing their local, internal, power being seriously threatened by revolutionary stirrings among the slaves and poor whites.

The Northern allies of the slavocracy, represented by papers like the New York *Herald* and the Chicago *Democrat*, warned that secession would mean abolition. Southern papers like the Nashville *Republican Banner* of January 26, 1861, declared that "Disunion [would be] the doom of slavery," while the Louisville *Daily Journal* of the same day felt that "Disunion" [was] the necessary antecedent of abolition." Two weeks later the Raleigh, North Carolina *Standard* warned that in a civil war the slaves "will become restless and turbulent.... The masses will at length rise up and destroy everything in their way.... The end will be—Abolition!"

In other words, certain leaders within the South were aware that docility and contentment were not characteristic of the Negro slave. And these men accurately foretold the future: the slaves did, in the Civil War, find and grasp their great opportunity to achieve that for which they had always fought—freedom.

Let us examine in detail the methods by which the Negro people helped to achieve this great end.

II. NON-SLAVE STATES

Notwithstanding the strategic declaration of the Republican Party that an intact union was the sole aim in the Civil War, Abolitionists, both Negro and white, promptly saw that the slaveholders' rebellion was the slaves' great opportunity. They therefore immediately agitated for the right of the Northern Negro to take an active, direct part in the destruction of the Confederacy. In 1861, Negroes in New York City formed themselves into a military club and held regular drill, until stopped by the police, in anticipation of fighting with the Federal forces. In Pennsylvania Governor Curtin refused an offer from free Negroes to go into the South and stir up slave revolts. It is certain, too, that some Negroes, passing themselves off as whites, served and fought with the Union armies from the opening of the war.

Just a few days after the fall of Fort Sumter, a free Negro of Washington, D. C., Jacob Dodson, offered his services and those of three hundred other Negroes for the Union army, but this was refused (April 29, 1861). Later during the same year another Negro, a physician of Battle Creek, Michigan, G. P. Miller, made a similar offer, but it also was rejected.

The presence and agitation of the Negroes were proving embarrassing to certain Republican leaders who were intent upon preventing open rebellion among Northern Democrats and border state inhabitants; therefore, propaganda in favor of Negro colonization in Africa became very prominent. Indeed the government set up a colonization department to carry through the idea. But, as earlier in our history, the movement collapsed because of the hostility of those who were to be colonized. Robert Purvis, a Philadelphia Negro, declared in August, 1862, that the Negroes would not leave:

. . . we were born here, and here we choose to remain. . . . We were coaxed and mobbed, and mobbed and coaxed; but we refused to budge . . . this is our country as much as it is yours, and we will not leave it.

However, Purvis added, the Negroes were ready and eager to fight for their country.

It was in that same month, August, 1862, that the Federal government made its first hesitating movements towards the enlistment of Negroes. And, notwithstanding very considerable discriminations, to be detailed elsewhere, over eighty-two thousand Northern Negroes fought for the Union forces.

Negroes were the leaders in the recruiting of their own people. An Ohio Negro leader, John M. Langston, declared: "Pay or no pay, let us volunteer." The Negroes felt this way because, as Frederick Douglass (whose two sons were among the first to enlist) stated:

Never since the world began was a better chance offered to a long enslaved and oppressed people. The opportunity is given us to be men. With one courageous resolution we may blot out the handwriting of the ages against us.

It was, too, the agitation of the same Negroes, people like Frederick Douglass, Lunsford Lane, Austin Steward, Peter Still, Charles Remond, Robert Purvis, together with white progressives like Horace Greeley, Elizur Wright, Gerrit Smith, Wendell Phillips—that was of very considerable importance in bringing about the issuance of the preliminary Emancipation Proclamation on September 22, 1862.

III. LOYAL BORDER STATES

The slaves in the loyal border states, Missouri, Kentucky, Maryland, did not permit the Federal government to go on believing it was fighting merely for the perpetuation of the Union; they persisted in considering its forces as the harbingers of freedom. They flocked to the colors by the tens of thousands, and even adverse army rulings —culminating in November, 1861, in an order refusing admittance to any more fugitives and turning out those already received (if not employed by the army)—did not effectively dampen the enthusiasm of the slaves for the Yankees. The rank and file of the army men never did fully enforce the obnoxious order of November, and this, together with the undiminished fleeing of thousands of slaves, led to its practical revocation in July, 1862. After this, slavery in the border states became more and more of a baseless structure.

As an example, let us examine in some detail the state of affairs in Missouri. In 1860 that state contained about 112,000 slaves. At the end of 1862 but 85,000 were left, some 5,000 having been forcibly sent South by their owners, and about 22,000 having escaped. With a more sympathetic Federal policy in the following months, it was simply impossible to hold the Negroes in bondage, so that in 1864 there were not more than 22,000 slaves left in the state. Mirroring the insecurity of that type of property, prices fell very rapidly, so that while the price of a good male slave had been $1,300 in 1860 it was but $100 in 1864. No wonder, then, that the slave state of Missouri officially abolished slavery (January 11, 1865) eleven months before the Federal government; the slaves had simply disappeared, into Kansas, Indiana, Illinois, and over 8,000 into the Federal army.

Similar conditions prevailed in Kentucky and Maryland. Well over 100,000 slaves fled their borders and more than 32,000 of them enlisted in the Army of the Republic.

Slavery was crumbling before the war broke out, and with the start of the armed conflict slavery was doomed. Whether emancipation was proclaimed or not, nothing could now hold the Negroes in bondage. The death of slavery within the border states, where the Proclamation of Emancipation did not apply, is convincing proof of that fact.

IV. THE CONFEDERATE STATES

But the great bulk of the Negro population, almost four million men, women and children (of whom 260,000 were free) lived within the Confederacy and, indeed, formed over forty per cent of the total population. It is impossible to understand the outcome of the Civil War without examining the behavior of that forty per cent, and the behavior of the Confederate government with regard to it.

WAS THE SOUTH UNPROTECTED?

Let it be immediately understood that the conventional story about the unprotected condition of the slave South is utter poppycock.

Slave laws and customs provided for division between domestic and field slaves, and between the field drivers or foremen and the rank and file workers. No slave could testify against a white, no slave might resist a white, no slave might go anywhere, or buy anything or sell anything without his owner's written permission. No slave was to carry arms of any kind. No slave was to be taught or learn how to read or write, and all writing and talking with a "tendency" to create disaffection was strictly forbidden. No assembling of slaves was allowed without express permission from the authorities, who uniformly required whites to be present. Every plantation with a certain number of slaves (varying from twenty to about fifty, according to place and time) was to have at least one adult white male upon it, and every rural district within the South was to be patrolled at stated periods (usually once in two or four weeks) by bodies of armed, mounted men. Every city had its patrol and guard and Negro curfew hour. Militia and volunteer military groups of a high degree of efficiency pervaded the slave area and saw frequent service in suppressing or overawing slave rebelliousness. The old Southern titles of Colonel and Major were not used merely for euphony or from politeness, but represented real military proficiency. Espionage and a religion with one message—docility—aided in the enslavement of the Negro people.

All this, in tightened form, and more, prevailed throughout the Confederacy during the war years.

The slavocracy invoked its religion with redoubled assiduity and warned its victims time without number of the dire sin of flaunting its rule; be meek and obedient. The whites attended the open religious meetings of the slaves and were pleased to hear prayers for the Confederacy, uttered, as the slaves knew, with tongue in cheek. Once when a Negro preacher prayed for the slavocracy with marked vehemence and apparently with great sincerity, his slave brethren, after the services, reproached him as a traitor. He replied: "Don't worry children; the Lord knew what I was talking about." But in the depth of the night and within their hovels, the slaves prayed for, and indeed, often to, Abraham Lincoln, so that, as a Negro remarked, "If the prayers that have gone up for the Union army could be read out you would not get through them these two weeks."

The favorite espionage method among the Confederates was for men to dress in the uniform of the Federal army and go among slaves asking for aid or information. And, too often, the slave would be deceived and furnish either or both, whereupon he would, most unceremoniously, be hanged.

Safeguards prevalent in the pre-war South were added to and strengthened. In the first conscription act of the Confederacy, passed in 1862, a provision exempted one adult male, owner or overseer, for every twenty slaves. In March, 1864, notwithstanding the fact that man-power was then Secessia's crucial problem, it was found necessary to exempt one white male for every fifteen slaves. These provisions not only weakened the Confederacy by withdrawing thousands of potential soldiers, but they were important factors in arousing the resentment of the poor, non-slaveholding whites, and helped to convince them that they were engaged in a "poor man's fight and a rich man's war."

Patrol laws were tightened. Thus in Florida, in December, 1861, it was decreed that the patrol was to perform its duties at least once every week, instead of every other week as before the war. Texas, in January, 1862, passed a similar law. Georgia, in 1862, cancelled all patrol exemptions and Louisiana the same year stiffened the penalty for failure to perform patrol duty, which, again, was to be performed at least once each week.

Moreover, throughout the war the states of the Confederacy maintained their own home guards, or state troops, which were separate from the militia and regular Confederate army. A major purpose and function of this organization was the maintenance of slave subordination. Appreciation of the necessity for these home guards helps explain the states' rights apologia, maintained by men like Governor Joseph Brown of Georgia, who time and again refused or impeded the use of Georgia's troops outside the state's own borders. These local guards, almost totally out of the fighting with the Federal army, numbered over 100,000 men, with 40,000 in Virginia, 20,000 in North Carolina, 23,000 in Tennessee and 18,000 in South Carolina.

Nor does that complete the story, for the Confederate army itself often assigned scouting parties to slave suppression or runaway apprehension duties, while the pickets of its army were much engaged, sometimes in pitched battles, with fugitive or turbulent slaves. At times, too, officers sent detachments from their regiment to certain areas, at the appeal of local authorities, for the same purposes, as into the neighborhood of Jackson, Mississippi, in October, 1862, and into Putnam county, Florida, in April, 1863.

Special safeguards were taken with the approximately 20,000 slaves conscripted by the Confederacy for labor in the army. The precautions were indeed so severe and so numerous as seriously to undermine the efficiency of a very unwillingly granted labor. First, every owner whose slaves were conscripted might (and many did) send their own overseer to help manage the slaves. Second, the government provided one Negro driver or foreman for every twenty-five slaves. Third, this driver was managed by a white overseer, one for every fifty slaves. And the overseer was directed by a manager, one for every one hundred slaves; and the manager was subordinate to a superintendent, one for every eight hundred slaves; and the superintendent was controlled by a director, one for every twenty-four hundred slaves. And yet, with all this, other precautions were taken—as when, for example, the Confederate Secretary of War placed a force of cavalry around a body of slaves laboring on a railroad and when an army officer in Texas placed the slaves under lock and key and a heavy guard in the evenings!

Nevertheless, the Confederate General Joseph E. Johnston declared in January, 1864, that he had "never been able to keep the impressed Negroes with an army near the enemy. They desert." Others suddenly developed all sorts of mysterious illnesses and pains that, it was observed, quite as suddenly disappeared if they managed to reach the Union forces. For example, from November, 1862, to January, 1863, there were 2,833 slaves conscripted for fortification work in Charleston, yet within that three-month period, 843, or thirty per cent, were already reported as "sick and runaway."

The Negro slaves within the plantations and cities of the Confederacy made themselves as trying and terrifying as they could.

STRUGGLES AGAINST ENSLAVEMENT

All through the period of slavery there had occurred strikes among groups of slaves who refused to work until certain conditions, such as a change in overseers, or better food, or shorter hours, were provided; and notwithstanding the ferocity of the punishment this entailed, the slaves sometimes won their demands. The same thing happened, and happened often, during the Civil War, with, at times, the addition by the slaves of a significant demand, the payment of wages. This was particularly prevalent in Louisiana in the summer of 1862, and in a few instances this demand was actually granted—abolition via the strike tactic. A more frequent occurrence was the cessation of physical punishment because of the strike or terror tactics of the slaves.

Sabotage, the maltreatment of work animals (this practice, as Karl Marx mentions in the first volume of *Capital*, is an important reason for the use of the mule and not the horse in the South), the destruction of tools, ruining of the crop, breaking of fences, shamming illness, were common phenomena throughout the slave period and were exceedingly prevalent within the Confederate states. One slaveholder in Texas in 1863, greatly alarmed at these practices, changed overseers and hired a brute, who beat

176

the slaves unmercifully and even shot at them; but the owner felt the slaves were even less subdued than before and decided to dismiss "this old fool" overseer. "The black wretches [were] trying all they can, it seems to me, to agrivate me, taking no interest, having no care about the future, neglecting their duty." This slaveholder, in desperation no doubt, even seriously contemplated getting rid of the slaves and actually working "with my hands!"

Another method by which the slaves who did not succeed in fleeing furthered the Federal cause was in the aid which they rendered to Union spies, Confederate deserters (who, before the war ended, numbered 100,000 men) and hundreds of escaped Yankee prisoners. This aid took the forms of valuable military information, of shelter, food, clothes, directions, and even, at times, money.

The evidence is clear and unquestionable on these points but is particularly abundant as regards the aid rendered hundreds of escaped Yankee prisoners. One of these men declared "that it would have been impossible for our men, held as prisoners of war in the South, to make an escape without the aid of Negroes." But not one was betrayed because, as another escaped prisoner declared, "The Negroes said they thought it their duty to do all they could for the Yankees, since massa Lincum and the Yankees were doing so much for them." At the risk of their lives, the slaves nursed the Yankees, and held secret meetings of dozens and scores of slaves, where their resources and knowledge were pooled; the prisoners—refreshed, fed, clothed, informed—went on as directed to the next group of slaves, and so on, until Mr. Lincoln's army received unexpected additions to its force.

This aid to Federal refugees is an interesting commentary on how shallow was the impression made on the slaves by the stories told them by their masters, that the Yankees were monsters with horns and tails, whose motive in coming South was to capture the slaves and sell them into Cuba. One alert ten-year-old Negro lad, who was aware that the slaves on his plantation were sheltering one such devil, turned these stories to good account when he was accosted by Confederate soldiers and asked if he had seen the Yankee. "Gor a'mighty, massa," said the youngster, "if dar was, you wouldn't catch dis darkey yer no how. Dem Yankees got horns on, massa, and I'se 'fraid of them. Ef I seed one of 'um coming for me, I'd die shoore."

Many of the slaves who remained on the plantations and in the towns of the Confederacy took the customary forms of expressing their hatred of slavery—assassination, arson, conspiracy. For the first item it is possible only to note that the record of American slavery is marked by innumerable killings of owners and overseers, and that the years of the Civil War by no means saw an end of this. On the contrary, the evidence indicates that this form of protest, like the others, occurred more frequently than ever before. Certainly at least one very intelligent English observer, William Howard Russell, noticed its great frequency in the very first year of the war.

Arson was another device frequently resorted to by America's slaves (who found it most difficult to obtain arms); and this, too, was attempted often in the Confederacy. However, it should be observed that the years of the war saw tremendous rebellious activity among the poor whites and Unionists within the South, and no doubt some of this incendiarism was due to them. But when a resident of Columbia, South Carolina, writes March 17, 1862—"Last night a house was set on fire; last week two houses. ... Our troubles thicken, indeed, when treachery comes from that dark quarter"—it seems plain that the suspected group is the slave population. Other explicit evidence shows incendiary activities among slaves in Louisiana and South Carolina in 1861, in Kentucky in 1862, and in Virginia in 1864. Indeed, in January, 1864, Jefferson Davis's own domestic slaves, with the connivance and aid of at least one other slave, set fire to his official residence in Richmond, and this was discovered none too soon for the health of the President of the Confederate States.

The Southern press was always exceedingly stingy with the space it allotted to accounts of slave disaffection, and this censorship was redoubled during the Civil War. Moreover, Northerners no longer traveled in, or communicated from, the South and thus another important source of news of slave difficulties was cut off.

Nevertheless about twenty-five distinct plots or hastily suppressed uprisings may be traced, though too often very little more than the date and place of occurrence are known. This is entirely apart from such general references as the following, contained in a letter of May 30, 1861, from a resident of New Orleans to the London *Daily News:* "There have been very alarming disturbances among the blacks; on more than one plantation, the assistance of the authorities has been called in to overcome the open resistance of the slaves";—or a letter from the Confederate General Daniel Ruggles, of October 3, 1862, from Jackson, Mississippi, asking the War Department for men for the more efficient control of the slaves since "pernicious influences have already been manifested upon many of these plantations...." One would wish the General had particularized these manifestations. Similarly there is a letter from Cherry Hill, South Carolina, dated March 27, 1863, which states: "There is a great and increasing disaffection among the Negroes"; but again no details are given.

With the opening of the fatal year 1861, and prior to the formal outbreak of hostilities, plots were exposed. The arrest of "several slaves" for "conspiring to form an insurrection" occurred in January in Manchester, Virginia. Later the same month a plot was uncovered in Columbia, South Carolina, and at least one white person, a German stone-cutter, was involved. Early in March the Atlanta, Georgia, *Intelligencer* reported "news from McKinley, Alabama, that a most damnable plot has been detected"; and again whites were declared to be implicated. Later that same month a plot was uncovered in the district of Prince George, South Carolina, "the ramifications of which extended for miles round, and in which the servants [slaves] of some score of planters were concerned."

Immediately following the start of the war, at the end of April, 1861, in a region declared to be some forty miles from Charleston, S. C., "an attempt at insurrection was put down ... and seven Negroes were hung." In Maryland, that very month, General B. F. Butler, of the still proslavery federal government, offered to put down a rumored slave uprising. In April and May there was what appears to have been serious trouble in Owen and Gallatin counties, Kentucky, where again whites were implicated. In May a plot among slaves in Louisiana, to have matured on July 4, was uncovered and crushed, and yet again whites were involved. The first week in June another slave conspiracy, which called for the sparing of the white children and women, was discovered in Monroe county, Arkansas, and the executions of four rebels—a Negro girl, two male slaves and a white man—were reported. At the same time the neighborhood of Brandon, Mississippi, was thrown into a panic by the discovery of a plot, and the execution of six slaves, by burning, was reported. At the end of July reports of trouble came from Jonesborough, Tennessee, but details are unknown. A lady in Charleston, South Carolina, declared, in a letter of November 23, 1861, that one of the greatest fears in the neighborhood was slave rebellion:

No general insurrection has taken place, though several revolts have been attempted; two quite recently, and in these
cases whole families were murdered before the slaves were
subdued. Then came retaliation of the most frightful character. . . . This news is suppressed as far as possible, and kept
entirely from the papers, for the Negroes hear what is published if they do not read it, and such examples might produce
disastrous consequences.

In Mississippi, July, 1862, there were two outbreaks
among slaves, resulting in the death of at least one white
man. A fugitive slave from this area told, early in August,
of conspiracies in central Mississippi and declared that an
unknown number of the rebels were burned alive. There is
evidence of very considerable unrest in Louisiana throughout the latter half of 1862. Federal generals stationed at
New Orleans took a most unfriendly attitude toward the
efforts of the slaves for freedom, imprisoning and returning thousands of fugitives, using a gunboat to overawe
rebellious slaves some twenty miles north of the city in
August, and loudly lamenting a slave revolt in November
which resulted in the severe injury of three white men,
about twenty miles from New Orleans. One general,
Weitzel, actually refused a command of Negro troops in
November because of the terror that it would arouse
among the enemy! Early in October an extensive conspiracy was disclosed in and around Culpeper county, Virginia. Free Negroes as well as slaves were implicated.
Seventeen rebels were executed. Northern newspapers
with reprints of the but recently issued Emancipation
Proclamation were discovered on the Negroes, and the
consternation was very great.

A rebellion in northern Mississippi around Holly
Springs was suppressed by Confederate troops in February, 1863.

In April, 1863, plots among the slaves of Putnam

county, Florida—aimed, it was thought, only at fleeing
—were reported, and Confederate soldiers were sent there
to aid in uncovering its ramifications. The Confederate
officer, Captain Chambers, in charge of this detachment,
was expressly told not to hesitate to arrest any whites who
might be implicated. In May disaffection among the slave
laborers in the furnaces of the key Tredegar Iron Works
of Virginia was suppressed. We are told only that "the
leaders were punished," but how many or in what manner
is not known. At the end of this month Governor Vance
of North Carolina sent captured plans to President Davis,
said to have originated among officers of the Federal government for a general slave revolt, to start August 1, 1863.
This was called to the special attention of the Secretary
of War and sent to General Robert E. Lee, but, so far as
is known, nothing came of it. About eighteen leaders of
a slave plot were arrested in Hancock county, Georgia,
in October, 1863; and except for these bare facts, nothing
more is known. And nothing more than the existence of
alarm over the behavior of slaves in Alabama in November, 1863, is recorded. Similarly great fears of slave rebellion prevailed in Kentucky in December, 1863, but their
bases are not clear.

Here is a typical example of the manner in which a
Confederate newspaper reported a slave plot. The Richmond *Examiner* of June 13, 1864, contains this item:

SERIOUS CHARGE AGAINST A NEGRO

A Negro named Bob Richardson, well known in Richmond
as a waiter in the saloons, has been committed to Castle
Thunder upon the charge of being at the head of a servile
plot which received its inspiration from the enemy, and which
was broken in upon a few days ago by the detectives. He will
receive his deserts right speedily.

And that is all there is.

In August, 1864, "manifestations of insubordination and rebellion among the Negroes" were reported from Bolivar county, Mississippi. In the same month a plot was discovered in Brooks county, Georgia. Within one day a public meeting was held and an examining committee of twelve citizens was formed. It performed its duties, and three slaves and one white man were hanged. A revolt of about thirty slaves in September in Amite county, Mississippi, was put down by a body of Confederate soldiers, and most of the rebels killed. Near Troy, Alabama, in December, 1864, an extensive slave conspiracy, which involved poor whites as well, was uncovered and crushed, but the results in human terms were never recorded.

In addition to the activity of the slaves who remained slaves—sabotage, strike, aid to enemies of the Confederacy, conspiracy and rebellion—undoubtedly the most disastrous blows that the Negro people delivered against that government came from the successful flight of hundreds of thousands (500,000 would appear to be a fair estimate) of these hewers of wood and drawers of water, and from their activities, when actually out of slavery, as guides, scouts, spies, pilots, laborers, fighters.

OUTLAW COMMUNITIES

America's slavocracy had always been troubled by groups of slave banditti, as they were called, formed by courageous runaway slaves, men, women, and children, who lived in the woods and swamps and mountains of the South and served as bases to which other slaves might flee, and from which the outlaws, the guerrillas, might attack the slaveholders and their employees. They existed during the Civil War and, it is interesting and important to note, often fought together with the thousands of outlaw poor whites, deserters and Unionists, who seriously menaced the slave government in every Southern state.

Such a group of runaway slaves, together with at least two whites, was, early in March, 1861, reported as harassing the planters around the Comite River in Louisiana. An armed expedition was sent out against them, but with what results is not known. A fairly full account of an outlawed community may be found in the Marion, South Carolina, *Star* of June 18, 1861:

RUNAWAYS

Last Tuesday a party of gentlemen from this place went in search of runaways who were thought to be in a swamp two miles from here. A trail was discovered which, winding about much, conducted the party to a knoll in the swamp on which corn, squashes, and peas were growing and a camp had been burnt. Continuing the search, another patch of corn, etc., was found and a camp from which several Negroes fled, leaving two small Negro children, each about a year old. . . . There were several guns fired at the Negroes who fled from the camp but none proved effectual. The camp seemed well provided with meal, cooking utensils, blankets, etc. The party returned, having taken two children, twelve guns and one axe. . . . Means should immediately be taken for the capture of these runaways, as they are probably lurking about this place.

In the neighborhood of Surry county, Virginia, in October, 1862, at least three whites were killed in an unsuccessful attack upon a group of about one hundred outlawed slaves—men, women and children.

And a Richmond newspaper, the *Examiner*, of January 14, 1864, referring to Camden and Currituck counties, North Carolina, declared,

. . . it is difficult to find words of description . . . of the wild and terrible consequences of the Negro raids in this obscure

... theater of the war. ... In the two counties ... there are said to be from five to six hundred Negroes, who are not in the regular military organization of the Yankees, but who, outlawed and disowned by their masters, lead the lives of banditti, roving the country with fire and committing all sorts of horrible crimes upon the inhabitants. ... This present theater of guerrilla warfare has, at this time, a most important interest for our authorities. It is described as a rich country ... and one of the most important sources of meat supplies that is now accessible to our armies.

This Confederate newspaper then goes on to suggest ever so faintly that "disloyal" whites were cooperating with the Negro "banditti."

There are other occasional contemporary allusions to the activities of these guerrillas, as the hanging of a Negro "renegade," or the killing of Confederate army pickets or of members of a patrol, particularly while in the act of apprehending runaways.

And in references to white guerrilla armies, the presence of Negro allies is at times noticed. Thus the Confederate general, R. F. Floyd, in a letter of April 11, 1862, asked the Governor of Florida to declare martial law in six Northeastern counties as "a measure of absolute necessity, as they contain a nest of traitors and lawless Negroes." The Governor of Alabama, J. G. Shorter, requested reinforcements from the Secretary of War to be sent to the southeastern counties of his state for, "the country near the coast is the common retreat of deserters from our armies, tories [!—Unionists] and runaway Negroes." Similar conditions existed in parts of Arkansas and Tennessee. A Union military report of August, 1864, stated that "500 Union men, deserters, and Negroes [were]...raiding towards Gainsville," Florida. That same month a Confederate General, John K. Jackson, reported from Lake City, Florida:

Many deserters . . . are collected in the swamps and fast-nesses of Taylor, La Fayette, Levy and other counties, and have organized, with runaway Negroes, bands for the purpose of committing depredations upon the plantations and crops of loyal citizens and running off their slaves. These depre-datory bands have even threatened the cities of Tallahassee, Madison and Marianna.

It may be noted here that further indication of unity between Southern poor whites and Negroes comes from the state of South Carolina itself. In the southeastern sec-tion of that state, after occupation by Federal troops, a convention was assembled, April 17, 1864, to participate in the election of delegates to a forthcoming presidential convention. The call for this convention invited all to par-ticipate without distinction of color. About two hundred and fifty people assembled, of whom one hundred and fifty were Negroes, and this convention selected sixteen delegates, of whom four were Negroes.

But undoubtedly the great bulk of the vast multitude of humanity that fled wherever freedom loomed went into Northern regions, especially the District of Columbia, Kansas, Illinois, Ohio, Indiana, Pennsylvania, and into those Southern localities controlled by the Union forces. This exodus of a people in the face of terrible difficulties and heartbreaking disappointments is, without question, one of the most, if not the most, heroic mass adventures in the history of the American people.

Let us again indicate some of the difficulties. Every twenty, or, later, every fifteen slaves, were directed and guarded by one armed white man. Every stretch of terri-tory under Confederate jurisdiction was patrolled by mounted, armed men at least once each week. If danger brewed, the army of the Confederacy itself, as has been shown, took a hand in watchdog and bloodhound activi-ties. The approach of a Union force led to wholesale forced removal of the slave population away from the region of liberty. Freedom was often twenty, fifty, five hundred miles away, through swamps, across rivers, over mountains, with death lurking everywhere. Yet tens of thousands of families, old men and women, children and infants, as well as strong and able Negroes, *succeeded* (how many failed will never be known) in reaching the zone of freedom.

The slavocracy exerted itself to keep its victims ignorant and misinformed. Slave stealers had been a common phenomenon before the war, and the Negroes were now assured that the Yankees were on a mass slave hunt and, said the slaveholders, creatures that would do such a thing must be devils, not humans. A conscious effort was also made to keep all news from the slaves, so that, for example, William Henry Trescott, of Charleston, a former Assistant Secretary of State, spoke French at his dinner table, explaining: "We know the black waiters are all ears now, and we want to keep what we have to say dark."

HOW THE SLAVES GOT THEIR INFORMATION

Nevertheless, observers, South and North, were impressed with how well informed the slaves were. They almost instinctively knew that this tremendous war was their opportunity and that the men from the North would, willy-nilly, aid them. And they knew, too, their standing, at a certain time, in the eyes of a swiftly changing code of laws, the whereabouts of the Federal forces, and the relative position of the belligerents at a given moment. How did they get their information?

In the first place, within the South there had always been and were whites who despised slavery and the state based upon it. These men informed slaves of the issues, forged passes for them, and even, as in Richmond and

Savannah, organized and operated bootleg rings to aid in smuggling the slaves through to freedom. The bands of white deserters also often aided, as well as received aid, from the slaves.

Secondly, many of the 260,000 free Negroes of the South felt a natural and deep sympathy for their brothers in chains, and greatly aided them, by information and provision, to reach freedom. And though the slavocracy consciously strove to keep the slaves illiterate, they never wholly succeeded. Slaves who could read passed on information to the others. For example, the New York *Tribune* correspondent told, October 21, 1862, of the entrance into the Union lines in Virginia of a fugitive slave, on horseback, who brought important military information. The slave was questioned and it was discovered that he knew well the provisions of the very recently issued Emancipation Proclamation, having read it in a newspaper. He had, too, read the life of Frederick Douglass, a history of St. Domingo (where Negro slaves had succeeded, by force of arms, in obtaining their freedom and possession of the country) and the story of John Brown. Concerning the latter he said: "I've read it to heaps of the colored folks. Lord, they think John Brown was almost a God!" Yet his master was unaware that he could read. And when the Union forces in the South set up schools for the escaped slaves, they discovered that a number could read and write, and that a few had actually conducted schools for slaves, secretly, of course, within the slave area.

Lastly, information spread with amazing rapidity via the grapevine telegraph. This simply consisted of a code language which the Negroes could and did use with impunity within earshot of the slaveholders. A few of these key words are known; "grease" meant freedom or liberty, and "Old Ride-Up" meant Abraham Lincoln. The whereabouts of Old Ride-Up's men and the possibility and method of greasing at a given moment could be sent over the countryside in a very short time.

It should also be observed that the Union government consciously went about spreading news of the Emancipation Proclamation, entrusting this very important work particularly to the Negro soldiers. Thus General Rufus Saxton, a commander in South Carolina, assembled his Negro soldiers after the issuance of the definitive Proclamation, January 1, 1863, and said to them:

It is your duty to carry this good news to your brethren who are still in slavery. Let all your voices, like merry bells join loud and clear in the grand chorus of liberty—"We are free," "We are free"—until listening, you shall hear its echoes coming back from every cabin in the land—"We are free," "We are free."

This was dangerous but joyous work, and was efficiently done.

The Confederacy's policy of the forced evacuation of slaves from endangered territory was often desperately resisted by the Negroes. Some were shot or bayoneted, but many did get away. The retreating planters would then, at times, go to the length of burning their houses and crops in order to make it as difficult as possible for those slaves who had not been carried away. But even so there were always thousands of half-starved and half-naked men, women and children to greet the Federals on their march, guide them, lead them to provisions, and work and fight for them, or rather, for themselves. Thus a South Carolinian wrote March 18, 1862: "...the Negroes are the source of the greatest trouble. Many persons have lost them all"; or, on November 13, 1862: "The low country is annoyed beyond measure by steps necessary to secure the Negroes that are left, but a fragment at best."

A Confederate major reports to his superiors, June 6,

1863: "Mr. Lowndes' overseer came down and informed me that some of his Negroes were trying to escape. I immediately ordered a portion of Lieutenant Breeden's company to go with the overseer to prevent their leaving, who succeeded in bringing back about thirty." Two weeks later another Confederate officer reports: "We saw some of Blake's Negroes endeavoring to get to the ferry; we went back to the road to get the dogs to cut them off; some of the Negroes turned back."

During the first year of the war the fugitive slaves, apparently at the end of their pilgrimage when at the camps of the Yankees, would there often meet the heartbreaking news that they were not welcome. And they would find themselves driven out, or returned, or being hunted for by their masters within the confines of the Federal camp itself. This was done in May and June and July, 1861, by officers like McClellan, R. C. Schenck, and J. B. Fry. Even though a resolution of the House of Representatives of July 9, 1861, condemned this, it continued to be done by Sherman, Halleck, Burnside, Hooker and Buell, the latter as late as March 6, 1862, condemning the rank and file men in his army who sheltered the fugitives as "lawless and mischievous."

But that same year, forced by the proddings of progressives, Negro and white, the continued influx of thousands of fugitives, and military necessity—the attitude of the Federal government and its army changed. Grant, by the end of February, 1862, forbade slave catching or the returning of fugitives by his regiments. In July rebel property was confiscated, and in August, 1862, Negroes were accepted as soldiers in the armies of the United States. One month later the preliminary Proclamation of Emancipation was issued, under the drive of the same forces enumerated above; and then the wires of the grapevine telegraph hummed night and day from Virginia to

Florida and across to Texas and up into Tennessee, and the doom of slavery was sealed.

Journals and diaries of Southerners are full of the mass flight of the slaves and the consequent great damage to the crops. Newspapers grew frantic at the disappearance of dozens of slaves every day from the cities, and the frontier counties of Virginia were exempted from the impressment act because the Confederacy had to depend on potential soldiers to raise food in that slave-denuded area.

Almost immediately after General Butler entered Fort Monroe in Virginia, fugitive slaves appeared. The first one came on May 24, 1861. Two days later eight more Negroes arrived. May 27, forty-seven fugitive slaves, men, women, and children, arrived. By July 30 there were nine hundred fugitive slaves within the Federal camp and, soon thereafter, the number ran into the thousands. Fort Monroe was now Fort Freedom, last stop on the "greasing" expeditions of thousands of Negroes from scores of miles around.

By 1862 a Confederate general was estimating that the state of North Carolina alone was losing one million dollars worth of slaves every week. And in August of that year a committee of citizens of Liberty (!) county, in Eastern Georgia, appealed to the Confederate officer in command, H. W. Mercer, to declare martial law in the region in order the more effectively to deal with the problem of runaway slaves. The committee's statement merits extensive quotation:

We allude to the escape of our slaves across the border lines landward, and out to the vessels of the enemy seaward, and to their being also enticed off by those who, having made their escape, return for that purpose, and not infrequently attended by the enemy. The injury inflicted upon the interests of the citizens of the Confederate States by this now constant drain is immense. Independent of the forcible seizure of slaves

191

by the enemy whenever it lies in his power, and to which we now make no allusion . . . we may set down as a low estimate the number of slaves absconded and enticed from our seaboard at 20,000, and their value at from $12,000,000 to $15,000,000, to which loss may be added the insecurity of the property along our borders and the demoralization of the Negroes that remain, which increases with the continuance of the evil, and may finally result in perfect disorganization and rebellion. The absconding Negroes hold the position of traitors, since they go over to the enemy and afford him aid and comfort by revealing the condition of the districts and cities from which they come.

Moreover, said the committee, the fugitives labor for the Union forces and are soon to be used as soldiers in the same cause:

Negroes occupy the positions of spies also, since they are employed in secret expeditions for obtaining information . . . and act as guides . . . and as pilots. . . . They have proved of great value thus far to the coast operations of the enemy.

The committee then declared that the citizens of an adjoining county had recently executed two slaves caught attempting to flee and that this summary procedure had had a very salutary effect upon the rest of the servile population. Won't you please, it urged, declare martial law in our region so that we too may have a "few executions of leading transgressors" and thus perhaps stem the wholesale flight of our workers?

THE NEGROES AS WORKERS AND SCOUTS FOR THE UNION

But more of that later. Let us now see what these runaway slaves did. Not only did they weaken the Confederacy; they also strengthened the Federal forces. First, thousands of these fugitives labored, either in Northern areas or in occupied Southern territory, in all sorts of occupations of importance to the Union—communications, mining, agriculture, manufacturing. And at least two hundred thousand Negroes, most of them former slaves, were directly connected with the Federal army as laborers, serving as teamsters, cooks, carpenters, nurses, fortification builders.

Thirdly, an unknown number, not regularly attached to the armed forces, served as spies and guides, providing eyes and ears for the strangers. A few examples of this may be given. Here is an item from Virginia (July 31, 1862): "Two contrabands [fugitive slaves] were sent on an important reconnaissance yesterday to a certain quarter. They escaped into our lines by making good use of their legs, and brought with them valuable information." An item of August 4, 1862, from Norfolk, tells of the exposure of three Confederate spies by fugitive slaves. Three days later we learn that a lost detachment of Union soldiers were taken back to their regiment by a slave. The Petersburg, Virginia, *Express* of August 9, 1862, lamented the frustration of a Confederate surprise attack "through the perfidy of a Negro, who gave information to the Yankee commander of our movements."

Confederate General W. S. Walker, writing in June, 1863, from McPhersonville, South Carolina, told of a particularly bold Union attack and declared: "Several intelligent Negroes had recently escaped to the enemy, among them a pilot...thoroughly familiar with the river. This will account for the boldness and celerity of the enemy's movements."

In 1864 the Confederate General Winder urged severe punishment for a captured Negro guide because: "It is a matter of notoriety in the sections of the Confederacy where raids are frequent that the guides of the enemy are nearly always free Negroes and slaves."

Two of the most famous of these Negro spies and guides were James Lawson and that almost incredibly courageous woman, Harriet Tubman, both of whom time and again went into Confederate territory and returned with invaluable information and, often, with more fugitive slaves.

Some of the fugitives, particularly those from fortification work, escaped with valuable goods, such as tools, horses, or even guns and ammunition. Indeed Charleston fugitives in May, 1862, presented the Union forces with a completely equipped Confederate gunboat. The leader in this exploit, an exploit that captured the attention of the nation, was a slave pilot, Robert Smalls. With eight comrades and five women and three children, he stole onto an unprotected gunboat, the *Planter*, in Charleston harbor, and piloted it past the port's batteries by giving the proper signals. They then avoided bombardment from the blockading Union fleet by raising a white flag. The gunboat fought for the Union, and Robert Smalls' professional skill as a pilot, acquainted with Southern waters, was also of great value to the same cause.

THE NEGROES AS SOLDIERS

In August, 1862, a vacillating Federal government, bombarded by appeals from white and Negro leaders—like Wendell Phillips, Elizur Wright, Frederick Douglass, Robert Purviss—seeing slavery disappearing from the loyal border states, and appreciating the great military significance of thousands of strong black arms, initiated the enrollment of Negroes as soldiers in the Army of the Republic. One hundred and twenty-five thousand Negroes from the slave states served in the Federal armies. They, together with the eighty thousand from the North, fought in four hundred and fifty battles, with an inspiring and inspired courage that was of the utmost importance in bringing about the collapse of the Confederacy and the abolition of slavery.

For here were over two hundred thousand armed Negro men fighting within a state built upon and dedicated to the proposition that the Negro was, if at all a human being, an innately and ineradicably inferior one, fit only to be a slave. This was why—as the genius of Karl Marx early saw, "A single Negro regiment would have a remarkable effect on Southern nerves"—200,000 armed Negroes shattered the slavocracy's morale and tore away its foundation.

And the Negro soldiers of the Republic fought notwithstanding shameful discriminations and disadvantages. White soldiers received thirteen dollars a month, Negroes received but seven dollars (until July 14, 1864, when the pay was equalized, retroactively to January 1, 1864); there were enlistment bounties for white recruits, none for Negroes (until June 15, 1864); and there was no possibility for advancement into the ranks of commissioned officers for Negroes. Moreover, the military policy of the terrified Confederate government was particularly brutal against its Negro adversaries. The Confederacy never recognized captured Negro soldiers who had been slaves as prisoners of war, and did not accord this status to captured free Negroes until October, 1864. The Negroes were either killed, returned to slavery, or confined at hard labor.

The Confederate General Mercer reported the capture in November, 1862, of four Negro soldiers and suggested that they be shot. The Secretary of War, James A. Seddon, gave him authority to do this.

President Jefferson Davis, in December, 1862, declared that all Negroes captured with arms were to be turned over to the state authorities and dealt with as insurrectionary slaves. The Confederate General Taylor, in June, 1863, reporting an engagement, stated significantly that he had "unfortunately" taken fifty Negro prisoners. General Kirby Smith hoped this was not true and that Taylor's officers "recognized the propriety of giving no quarter to armed Negroes and their officers. In this way we may be relieved from a disagreeable dilemma." The Secretary of War thought General Smith's policy too drastic but agreed that "a few examples" might well be made. About this time, the summer of 1863, the Confederacy began to report the shooting of Negro prisoners "while attempting to escape."

The Richmond *Enquirer* of December 17, 1863, stated the matter in a surprisingly frank way:

Should they [Negroes] be sent to field, and put in battle, *none will be taken prisoners* [italics in original]. Our troops understand what to do in such cases. If any Negroes have been captured during the war, as soldiers in the enemy's ranks, we have not heard of them. We do not think that such a case has been reported.

When a subordinate reported in March, 1864, to Colonel W. P. Shingler, the capture of four Negroes, he was directed to see to it that he made no such reports in the future. Other Negro prisoners were jailed or delivered back into slavery and, indeed, there is record of at least three Negroes, who had been free, having been sold into slavery when captured in the uniform of the United States.

The Negro soldiers and their friends, Negro and white, fought the discrimination vigorously by agitation and protest, and one Negro regiment, the 54th Massachusetts, served for an entire year but refused to be paid at all. An indication of the morale of the Negro soldiers lies in the fact that there was but one instance of mass disobedience, or mutiny, among the men of a Negro regiment. This occurred in December, 1863, in Louisiana in protest against their brutal Negro-hating commander, Lieutenant Colonel

Benedict. Seven of the soldiers were arrested, but because of the circumstances none was shot. Benedict was himself court-martialed and dismissed from the service for having inflicted "cruel and unusual punishment" upon his men.

The policy of frightfulness adopted by the Confederacy did nothing but convince the Negro fighters that the battle was to the death, and they fought accordingly. The testimony as to how well they fought is unanimous.

Here are a few of the tributes paid them by men who led them in action. On November 12, 1862, Brigadier General Rufus Saxton reported: "It is admitted upon all hands that the Negroes fought with a coolness and bravery that would have done credit to veteran soldiers. There was no excitement, no flinching, no attempt at cruelty when successful. They seemed like men who were fighting to vindicate their manhood and they did it well."

On November 22, 1862, Lieutenant Colonel O. T. Beard wrote: "On the last expedition the fact was developed that colored men would fight behind barricades; this time they have proved, by their heroism, that they will fight in the open field." On March 14, 1863, Rufus Saxton again reported: "... in every action the Negro troops have behaved with the utmost bravery. Never in a single instance have I learned that they have flinched."

General E. S. Dennis wrote on June 7, 1863: "It is impossible for men to show greater gallantry than the Negro troops." Similar testimony came from Generals Banks, L. Thomas, J. G. Blunt, S. A. Hurlbut, G. C. Strong, A. H. Terry, W. F. Smith, T. J. Morgan and Colonels J. A. Foster, D. G. Ader and J. A. Taylor.

General Ulysses S. Grant said little, but his action is quite eloquent. When, in 1864, he was made commanding general of the Union forces and transferred from the West to the decisive Virginia front, he insisted upon taking with him 20,000 Negro soldiers.

A Confederate soldier after a particular engagement exclaimed: "I never saw such disregard of danger and certain death as these Negroes displayed." The Richmond *Dispatch* of August 2, 1864, following another battle, also stood aghast at their astounding courage. Both the Southern soldier and the Southern editor could account for this only with the ridiculous explanation that the members of the regiments were drunk on both occasions!

Let us observe in some detail, as examples, two instances of the great courage of the Negro fighters. Early in 1863 the Confederate forces determined upon a desperate effort to recapture that tremendously important city, New Orleans. The key to that city was Ship Island. Ten Federal companies guarded it, three white and seven Negro. In April, 1863, this island was attacked by a Confederate force five times more numerous than the defenders. And Union gunboats sent to the aid of the besieged men actually and, it is believed, purposely shelled the Negro troops instead of the enemy. Nevertheless the Confederates were repulsed. The Federal commander declared, referring to the Negro soldiers: "They were constantly in the thickest of the fight, and by their unflinching bravery, and admirable handling of their commands...reflected great honor upon the flag."

A Union army laid siege to a strong Confederate force entrenched in Port Hudson, Louisiana, in May, 1863. Two Negro regiments were ordered to attack. They did—through direct and cross fire. General Banks reported:

The deeds of heroism performed by these colored men were such as the proudest white men might emulate. Their colors are torn to pieces by shot, and literally bespattered by blood and brains. The color-sergeant of the First Louisiana, on being mortally wounded, hugged the colors to his breast, when a struggle ensued between the two color-corporals on each side of him, as to who should have the honor of bearing the sacred standard, and during this generous contention, one was seriously wounded. One black lieutenant actually mounted the enemy's works three or four times, and in one charge the assaulting party came within fifty paces of them. Indeed, if only ordinarily supported by artillery and reserve, no one can convince us that they would not have opened a passage through the enemy's works.

In this effort to achieve the impossible the Negro troops made "six distinct charges" and fought "from morning until 3:30 P.M. under the most hideous carnage that man ever had to withstand."

Here were these scores of thousands of hitherto enslaved and oppressed masses, armed, and sent forth into their own country, whose every creek and knoll was known to them, maintain their newly obtained freedom, to prove their manhood, and to liberate their own people, their own parents and children and wives, from a slavery that they knew only too well. Hear the keen and heroic commander of a Negro regiment, Colonel Thomas Wentworth Higginson:

No officer in the regiment now doubts that the key to the successful prosecution of this war lies in the unlimited employment of black troops. Their superiority lies simply in the fact that they know the country, while white troops do not and, moreover, that they have peculiarities of temperament, position and motive which belong to them alone. Instead of leaving their homes and families to fight they are fighting for their homes and families, and they show that resolution and sagacity which a personal purpose gives. It would have been madness to attempt, with the bravest white troops what I have successfully accomplished with the black ones.

A recent and critical student of the question, Professor Fred A. Shannon, has succinctly summed up the matter: "There can be no question as to the value of the Negro soldiers in the war." Even the *Confederate Military His-*

tory, in its own inimitably bitter way, has declared: "The Negroes are entitled to the credit of vindicating the statement as to a military necessity for their enrollment to enable the Federal armies to match the Confederate." Finally, an individual who was in an excellent position to know the truth in this matter said, referring to the Negro soldiers: "Take two hundred thousand men from our side and put them in the battlefield or cornfield against us, and we would be compelled to abandon the war in three weeks." That was the opinion of Abraham Lincoln.

The Negro people, and all other Americans, should know and be proud of the fortitude displayed at Fort Wagner, Port Hudson and Petersburg, at Olustee, Ship Island and Bermuda Hundred, at Nashville, Fort Powhatan and Milliken's Bend. And let it always be remembered that in the war to save the republic thirty-seven thousand Negro soldiers were killed in action.

THE CONFEDERACY TRIES TO MAKE SOLDIERS OF ITS SLAVES

Excellent evidence of the effectiveness of the Negro soldier and of the desperation to which the Confederacy was driven largely by their activities of the slaves is to be seen in the movement within Secessia itself to emancipate and arm the slaves. The idea was first seriously discussed in the summer of 1863. It was brought to a head when, at that time, Confederate General Patrick R. Cleburne, a non-slaveholder, suggested in a written report to his comrades-in-arms the advisability and, indeed, necessity for the Confederacy to offer freedom and arms to able-bodied Negroes and to enroll them as soldiers. For, Cleburne rather hastily concluded, "as between loss of independence and the loss of slavery, every patriot would give up the latter." Moreover, he referred to the efficiency of the

Negro fighters in the Federal forces, and urged that if freed the slaves would "change from a dread menace to a position of strength." In other words the co-existence of slavery and the Confederate government was impossible; one had to go.

This proposal was then called incendiary and was suppressed; but by 1864 men like Edmund Ruffin, a pioneer Virginia secessionist (whose slaves had all fled), Judah Benjamin, Secretary of the Treasury, William Smith, Governor of Virginia, and Robert E. Lee were urging the same measures. Jefferson Davis had his agents feel out European powers as to their attitude if the slaves were freed.

It was understood that freedom was inseparable from, was a necessary concomitant of, the arming of the Negroes. As an Alabama legislator declared in 1864, were the South to enlist a quarter of a million slaves as soldiers, with no provision for their emancipation, "the South would lose 250,000 slaves—for not one would ever return." And after reiterating for generations what a boon slavery was and how happy in it the Negroes were, it was a very ticklish and embarrassing thing to admit that nothing but the granting of freedom would ever possibly get the Negroes to fight for the Confederacy. Said the Richmond *Enquirer* in 1864:

It should be remembered that whether freedom to the Negro be really a blessing or a curse, many Negroes desire it, and are willing to take it, even from the Yankees. Freedom is [to be] given to the Negro soldier, not because we believe slavery is wrong, but because we must offer to the Negroes inducements to fidelity which he regards as equal, if not greater, than those offered by the enemy.

By January, 1865, General Howell Cobb, of Georgia, who had been Buchanan's Secretary of the Treasury, was finding this in his mail:

We cannot get from the militia a sufficient number to recruit our army and if we could it would not do to take all the male population out of the country. . . . I see but one alternative left us and that to fill up our army with Negroes. . . . We are told however that they cannot be made to fight. They have done some very good fighting for the Yanks, and I cannot see why they will not do as well for us if we give them their freedom.

But Cobb, like Governor Joseph Brown of Georgia, felt that "if the Negro was fit to be a soldier, he was not fit to be a slave," and that the enlistment of Negroes would be the "beginning of the end of the [slaveholders'] revolution."

Similarly, the Richmond *Dispatch*, in November, 1864, opposed arming the Negroes, for that entailed freedom, and if that were granted, what, it wanted to know, were we fighting for anyway? Yet three months later it had reversed itself and came out for arming the Negroes, for it now felt that if emancipation were any longer delayed the last hope of the Confederacy was gone. The Negroes, in other words, *by their own struggles had, for all practical purposes, killed slavery*. Thus as Jefferson Davis himself stated in February, 1865: "All arguments as to the positive advantage or disadvantage of employing them are beside the question, which is simply one of relative advantage between having their fighting element in our ranks or in those of the enemy." And Robert E. Lee hoped he "could at least do as well with them as the enemy, and he attaches great importance to their assistance."

In March, 1865, the Confederate States of America announced to the world the destruction of its own base when, in a futile gesture, it passed a law calling for the enlistment of Negro slaves into its army as soldiers; and while the enactment was ambiguous as to emancipation, it was generally acknowledged that that was entailed. The enlistment proceeded very slowly indeed, and the act is merely symbolically significant, for within a month the Confederacy was totally crushed. The fact is that not one Negro soldier fired a shot for that creature raised up by his people's oppressors.

V. CONCLUSION

In the days when slavocracy was supreme in church and state and counting house, a preacher on a particular Sunday was demonstrating the divine sanction for human slavery. He scoffed at the Abolitionists as mere annoying insects, as mosquitoes. Harriet Tubman—who had been back and forth from the South to the North with a handful of rescued slaves so often that her people called her their Moses—arose, and in her shrill voice, announced: "That's so, we're mosquitoes; and we're going to keep right on stinging."

The American Negroes never let the world forget their oppression and enslavement. They purchased their freedom where possible, they killed themselves, they cut off their fingers and hands, they refused to work and were tortured. They fled to swamps and congregated and waged war, they fled to havens of liberty, to invading armies, to the Indians, to the Canadians, to the Dutch, to the French, to the Spaniards and Mexicans, and to the Northern states; and there they went from door to door seeking money wherewith to purchase the freedom of their parents or wives or children. They went from city to city, did these Negroes—Douglass, Still, Allen, Hall, Steward, Lane, Bibb, Northrup, Truth, Tubman, Walker, Garnet, Remond, Purvis and a thousand more—explaining, describing, pleading, warning, agitating. They wrote pamphlets and letters and books, telling of the plight of their people, and urging reform or rebellion. They plotted or rebelled, alone or with the poor whites, time and time again; and the corpses of the martyrs were barely cold before others sprang forward to give their lives' blood to the struggle— Denmark Vesey, Nat Turner and scores upon scores of plain Catos, Gabriels, Jacks, Arthurs, Toms, Peters, Sams, Tonys, Patricks, Greens, Copelands.

Finally, a bloodstained, militaristic oligarchy saw its national power ripped from it and its local, internal power seriously threatened by a revolution of its mudsill, its base. It rose in rebellion itself in a desperate attempt to stop the clock of history. *Its effort was foiled essentially because the internal revolt it foresaw occurred.* The poor whites fled from its armies and waged war upon it. The slaves conspired or rebelled, or broke its tools, or refused to do its work, or fled its fields and mines and factories. Many fought shoulder to shoulder with the Southern poor whites against a common enemy, and a multitude joined the army from the North and brought it information and guidance and labor and a desperate courage. Thus was American slavery crushed.

The deck was then cleared for further action. The nation was now unified and controlled by an industrial bourgeoisie based upon free wage-labor. The labor movement had an opportunity to develop unhindered by the obstacle of chattel slavery. In the classic formulation of Karl Marx, "Labor with a white skin cannot emancipate itself where labor with a black skin is branded."

There were, of course, immediate struggles and advances following the war (detailed and described in James S. Allen's *Reconstruction: The Battle for Democracy*). During the post-Civil War period, the Negro people, in alliance with the poor whites of the South and the radical bourgeois democrats of the North, secured the extension of suffrage, the establishment of a public school system for both races, and the greater distribution of land. These democratic advances were achieved only after the most bitter struggles, struggles in which, despite the traditional picture, the colored freedmen acted in an independent role.

But the heroic fight of the Negro people and their allies for democracy, land and civil rights in the South was defeated chiefly as a result of the shameful betrayal by the industrial and financial bourgeoisie of the North. In 1877 the latter came to an understanding with the reactionary plantocracy of the South. Working through the reactionary wing of the Republican Party, the Northern big bourgeoisie sold out the Revolution by giving the old slave oligarchy a free hand ("home rule") in the Southern states. This "gentlemen's agreement" meant disenfranchisement for the Negro, sharecropping peonage, lynch terrorism, and the loss of civil liberties and educational opportunities.

Yet, the fight for Negro rights was not ended by the Hayes-Tilden episode of 1877. It continued thereafter, and today is being carried on as never before with the aid of the labor and progressive movement. Based on the solid foundation of black and white unity, the present struggle for Negro rights is bound up with the battle for democracy. The alliance between Negro and white is a natural and firm one capable of accomplishing the unfinished tasks of revolutionary Reconstruction.

APPENDICES

CHRONOLOGY OF SLAVE REVOLTS

The following is a minimum list. Contemporary evidence has been examined for each of the revolts listed. Alleged revolts referred to in secondary works are not given here because the references were erroneous or doubtful. Censorship was rigid at that time and it is highly probable that some of the revolts were never reported. At times, too, slave disaffection was reported in such general terms that it is difficult to know whether concrete revolts were behind the generalities. Such cases are not listed below. An asterisk indicates that at least two revolts were reported within the given year and the indicated area.

Date	Locality
1526	S. C.
1644	Va.
1657	Conn.
1663	Va.
1672	Va.
1680s	Va., N. Y., Md.
1687	Va.
1688	Md.
1690s	Va., Mass.
1694	Va.
1702	N. Y., S. C.
1705	Md.
1708	N. Y.
1709	Va.
1710	Va.
1711	S. C.
1712	N. Y.
1713	S. C.
1720	S. C., Mass.
1721	S. C.
1722	Va.
1723	Va., Conn., Mass.
1727	La.
1729	Va.

Date	Locality
1730	Va., S. C., La.
1732	La.
1733	S. C.
1734	S. C., N. J.
1737	S. C., Pa.
1738	S. C., Md.
1739	S. C.,* Md.
1740	S. C.
1741	N. Y., N. J.
1744	S. C.
1747	S. C.
1755	Va.
1759	S. C.
1760	S. C.
1761	S. C.
1765	S. C.
1766	S. C.
1767	Va.
1768	Mass.
1770	Va.
1771	Ga.
1772	N. J.
1774	Ga., Mass.

Date	Locality	Date	Locality
1775	N. C., S. C.	1823	Va.
1776	Ga., N. J.	1824	Va.
1778	N. Y.	1825	N. C.
1779	Ga., N. J.	1826	Miss.
1782	Va., La.	1827	Ga., Ala.
1783	N. C.	1829	Ky., Va., S. C., N. C., Ga., La.
1784	La.	1830	Miss., Md., N. C., La., Tenn.
1786	Ga., Va.	1831	everywhere
1787	S. C.	1833	Va.
1791	La.	1835	Miss., S. C., Ga., La., N. C.,
1792	La., N. C., Va.		Tex., Md., Va.
1793	Va., S. C.	1836	Ga., Tenn., Mo., Va.
1795	La.,* N. C.	1837	La.
1796	N. C., S. C., Ga., N. J., N. Y.	1838	D. C., Ky., Tenn.
1797	Va., S. C.	1839	La., Tenn., Ga., Ky.
1798	S. C.	1840	La., Ala., D. C., N. C., Va.,
1799	Va.		Md.
1800	Va., N. C., S. C.	1841	La., Ga., Miss., Ala.
1801	Va.	1842	La., Tenn., Ala., Mo.
1802	Va.,* N. C.	1843	La.
1803	N. C., Pa.	1845	Md., La.
1804	Ga., La., Pa.	1848	Ky.*
1805	N. C., S. C., Va., Md., La.,	1849	Ga.
	Ga.	1850	Mo., Va.
1806	Va.	1851	Ga., La., N. C., Tex.
1807	Miss.	1852	Va.
1808	Va.	1853	La.
1809	Va., La.	1854	La.
1810	Va., Ga., Ky., N. C., Tenn.	1855	Md., S. C., Miss., La., Mo.,
1811	Va., La.*		Ga.
1812	Va., La., Ky., Miss.	1856	everywhere
1813	D. C., S. C., Va.	1857	Md.
1814	Md., Va.*	1858	Miss., Ark.
1816	Va., S. C.*	1859	Va.,* Mo.
1817	Md.	1860	everywhere
1818	N. C., Va.	1861	everywhere but N. C., Fla.,
1819	Ga., S. C.		Tex.
1820	Fla., Va., N. C.	1862	Miss.,* La., Va.
1821	N. C.	1863	Fla., Va., Ga., Ky., Miss.
1822	S. C.*	1864	Va., Miss.,* Ga., Ala.

There were also scores of revolts on slave ships, both domestic and foreign. At least two of these, that on the foreign trader *Amistad* (1839) and that on the domestic trader *Creole* (1841) attracted nationwide and international attention. In both cases the rebels secured their liberty.

BIBLIOGRAPHY

NEGRO SLAVE REVOLTS IN THE UNITED STATES, 1526-1860

SUGGESTED READING

The material in this booklet was mainly culled from highly dispersed, rare and out-of-the-way sources, such as contemporary newspapers, journals, diaries and memoirs. Much was obtained from manuscripts in the New York Public Library, the Congressional Library in Washington, and the Virginia (Richmond), North Carolina (Raleigh), and South Carolina (Columbia) state libraries and archives. Detailed references to these sources are impossible here.

Fairly complete references to published works on the subject will be found in the footnotes to the article by Harvey Wish in the *Journal of Negro History* (1937) XXII, pp. 299-320, and to the articles by the present writer in *Science and Society* (1937, 1938) I, pp. 512-38; II, pp. 386-92. The most complete bibliography will be found in the present writer's book, *American Negro Slave Revolts* (Columbia University Press, 1943). The book published in Boston, December, 1938—*Slave Insurrections in the United States, 1800-1865*, by Joseph C. Carroll—also contains considerable references, but the work is so full of errors, both of commission and of omission, that it cannot be unqualifiedly recommended.

THE NEGRO IN THE AMERICAN REVOLUTION

PRIMARY SOURCES

The writings of the following statesmen were useful (the names of the editors of the collections used are in parentheses): JOHN ADAMS (C. Adams); BENJAMIN FRANKLIN (A. Smyth); THOMAS JEFFERSON (P. Ford); RICHARD HENRY LEE (J. Ballagh); JAMES MADISON (G. Hunt); THOMAS PAINE (M. Conway); GEORGE WASHINGTON (J. Fitzpatrick).

Archives of Maryland, XXI, XLIII, XLVII.
Archives of New Jersey, Second series, I, II.
Archives of Pennsylvania, Fifth Series, IV, V.
BURNETT, EDMUND, ed., *Letters of Members of the Continental Congress*, 8 vols.

Calendar of Virginia State Papers, I, II, III.
CANDLER, ALLEN, ed., *Revolutionary Records of Georgia*, I.
CLARK, WALTER, ed., *State Records of North Carolina*, X, XI, XIV, XV, XIX, XXIV.
Collections of the Connecticut Historical Society, VIII, XII.
Collections of the Massachusetts Historical Society, Fifth series, III, pp. 432-37, "Negro petitions for freedom."
Documents in *Virginia Historical Magazine*, XIV, pp. 251, 385, 406-407.
Document in *William and Mary College Quarterly*, XVII, p. 236.
FERNOW, BERTHOLD, ed., *New York in the Revolution*, State Archives, I.
FORCE, PETER, ed., *American Archives*, 9 vols.
GOODRICH, JOHN, ed., *Rolls of the Soldiers in the Revolutionary War*, State of Vermont.
HAMMOND, ISAAC, ed., *Rolls of the Soldiers in the Revolutionary War*, State of New Hampshire, 4 vols.
HENING, WILLIAM, ed., *Statutes at Large of Virginia*, IX, X, XI, XII, XIII.
KNIGHT, LUCIAN, ed., *Georgia's Roster of the Revolution*.
Massachusetts Soldiers and Sailors of the Revolution, 17 vols.
MCILWAINE, H. R., ed., *Official Letters of the Governors of Virginia*, I, III.
PALTSITS, VICTOR, ed., *Minutes of the Commissioners for Detecting and Defeating Conspiracies in the State of New York*, 3 vols.
SPARKS, JARED, ed., *Correspondence of the American Revolution*, I, II, III.
SULLIVAN, JAMES, ed., *Minutes of the Albany Committee of Correspondence*, 2 vols.
WILLARD, MARGARET, ed., *Letters of the American Revolution*.

SECONDARY SOURCES

APTHEKER, H., "Negroes Who Served in Our First Navy," *Opportunity*, April, 1940.
HARTGROVE, W. B., "The Negro in the Army of the Revolution," *The Journal of Negro History* (1916), I, pp. 110-131.
LIVERMORE, GEORGE, *An Historical Research Respecting the Opinions of the Founders of the Republic on Negroes as Slaves, as Citizens, and as Soldiers*, Boston, 1862.
MOORE, GEORGE, *Historical Notes on the Employment of Negroes in the American Army of the Revolution*, N. Y., 1862.
NELL, WILLIAM, *The Colored Patriots of the Revolution*, Boston, 1855. This was written by a leading Negro Abolitionist who was a pioneer student of Negro history. It is at times inaccurate, but contains much of value.
TITTAMIN, WILLIAM, "The Negro in the American Revolution," unpublished master's thesis, New York University, 1939.
WILKES, LAURA, *Missing Pages in American History*, Washington, 1919.

Some local histories yielded considerable information. This was especially true of the following Massachusetts communities (the authors' names are in parentheses): Groton (S. GREEN); Hadley (L. BOTTWOOD); Lancaster (H. NOURSE); Malden (D. COREY); Middlesex County (S.

DRAKE); Northfield (J. TEMPLE and G. SHELDON); Palmer (J. TEMPLE); Pittsfield (J. E. SMITH); Worcester (W. LINCOLN).

The following state histories yielded the most material: S. G. ARNOLD, *Rhode Island*, II; E. M. COULTER, *A Short History of Georgia;* A. B. HART, ed., *Massachusetts*, III; IRVING KULL, *New Jersey*, II; D. D. WALLACE, *South Carolina*, II.

Of the biographical works those by JOHN BAKELESS on Daniel Boone; C. BOLTON and W. MAZYCK on Washingon; THOMAS COOLEY on Lemuel Haynes; FRANK HUMPHREYS on David Humphreys; WILLIAM D. JAMES on Francis Marion; WILLIAM JOHNSON on Nathanael Greene; and ALEXANDER GRAYDON's *Memoirs* were most important.

Other useful miscellaneous sources of information are:

ALLYN, CHARLES, *The Battle of Groton Heights*, New London, 1882.

APTHEKER, HERBERT, in *The Journal of Negro History* (1939), XXIV, p. 170.

APTHEKER, HERBERT, in *Science & Society* (1937), I, pp. 519, 537.

CHANNING, EDWARD, "The war in the southern department" in J. WINSOR, ed., *Narrative and Critical History of America*, VI, Boston, 1887.

DINIAN, J. L., in *Rhode Island Historical Tracts*, No. 1, Providence, 1877.

DODD, W. E., "Virginia takes the road to revolution," in DODD, CLARK, BECKER, *The Spirit of '76*, Washington, 1927.

FRIEDENWALD, HERBERT, *The Declaration of Independence*, N. Y., 1904.

GREENE, E. B., and V. HARRINGTON, *American Population Before 1790*, N. Y., 1932.

HARDY, JACK, *The First American Revolution*, N. Y., 1937.

KIDDER, F., *History of the Boston Massacre*, Albany, 1870.

KING, HENRY, *Sketches of Pitt County* (N. C.), Raleigh, 1911.

LOSSING, BENSON, *The Pictorial Field-book of the Revolution*, N. Y., 1860.

LOWELL, EDWARD, *The Hessians in the Revolutionary War*, N. Y., 1884.

MCCRADY, EDWARD, *The History of South Carolina in the Revolution*, N. Y., 1901.

OGG, FREDERICK, in *Annals of the American Historical Association*, 1901, I, pp. 275-298.

PHILLIPS, D., in *Journal of American History*, 1911, V, pp. 143-146.

RIDER, SIDNEY, in *Rhode Island Historical Tracts*, No. 10, Providence, 1880.

SIEBERT, WILBUR, *Loyalists in East Florida*, Deland, 1929, 2 vols.

STEWARD, T. G., in *American Negro Academy Papers*, No. 5, Washington, 1899.

SWETT, S., *Bunker Hill Battle*, Boston, 1818.

UPTON, RICHARD, *Revolutionary New Hampshire*, Hanover, 1936.

WOODSON, CARTER, *The Negro in Our History*, Washington, 1928.

THE NEGRO IN THE ABOLITIONIST MOVEMENT

For an extended bibliography, see the author's article, under the same title, in *Science and Society*, 1941, V, Nos. 1 and 2.

BUCKMASTER, HENRIETTA, Let My People Go, New York, 1941.

COFFIN, LEVI, *The Reminiscences of Levi Coffin*, Cincinnati, 1876.

DOUGLASS, FREDERICK, *The Life and Times of Frederick Douglass*, New York, 1941.

GROSS, BELLA, "Freedom's Journal and the Rights of All," *The Journal of Negro History*, XVII, 1932.

PORTER, DOROTHY B., "Afro-American Writings before 1835," unpublished master's thesis, Columbia University, 1932.

PORTER, DOROTHY B., "The Organized Educational Activities of Negro Literary Societies, 1828-1846," *The Journal of Negro Education*, V, 1936.

RICHARDSON, CLARICE A., "The Anti-Slavery Activities of Negroes in Pennsylvania," unpublished master's thesis, Howard University, 1937.

SIEBERT, WILBUR H., *The Underground Railroad*, New York, 1899.

STILL, WILLIAM, *Underground Railroad Records*, Philadelphia, 1886.

WESLEY, CHARLES, "The Negroes of New York in the Emancipation Movement," in *The Journal of Negro History*, XXIV, 1939.

WESLEY, CHARLES, *Richard Allen, Apostle of Freedom*, Washington, 1935.

WHITTAKER, HELEN B., "The Negro in the Abolition Movement," unpublished master's thesis, Howard University, 1935.

WOODSON, CARTER G., *The Negro in Our History*, Washington, 1941.

WOODSON, CARTER G., *The Mind of the Negro as Reflected in Letters Written During the Crisis, 1800-1860*, Washington, 1926.

WOODSON, CARTER G., *The Education of the Negro Prior to 1861*, New York, London, 1915.

THE NEGRO IN THE CIVIL WAR

BROWN, WILLIAM WELLS, *The Negro in the American Rebellion* (Boston, 1867). This book, by a one-time slave, deals with the military activities of the Negro.

BRUCE, KATHLEEN, *Virginia Iron Manufacture in the Slave Era* (N. Y., 1931). Some notice, in a rather condescending tone, is given to the slave labor and slave control problems in the very important Tredegar Iron Works during the war.

CARSON, JAMES P., *Life, Letters and Speeches of James Louis Petigru* (Washington, 1920). This contains excellent material on slave difficulties in South Carolina in personal letters from a wealthy slaveholder.

CHESNUT, MARY B., *A Diary from Dixie*, edited by J. D. Martin and M. L. Avary. Occasional revealing references to the Negro by the wife of a Confederate general who had been a senator from South Carolina.

CONWAY, MONCURE D., *Testimonies Concerning Slavery* (London, 1864).

This work, by a prominent Virginian, is of great general importance and is of specific value here for its evidence of how well informed the slaves were of the progress of the war.

COULTER, E. MERTON, *The Civil War and Readjustment in Kentucky* (Chapel Hill, 1926). Two pages (247-248) contain some material of value on the role of Kentucky's slaves.

CRAVEN, AVERY, *Edmund Ruffin* (N. Y., 1932). Clear evidence of the ruinous effects of the flight of the slaves on the agricultural foundation of the Confederacy is presented, rather incidentally, here.

DAVIS, WILLIAM W., *The Civil War and Reconstruction in Florida* (N. Y., 1913). One of the very few state monographs to even indicate a real awareness of the presence of Negro slaves. It contains valuable material.

DOUGLASS, FREDERICK, *Life and Times of Frederick Douglass*. The latter half of this book is important for this subject. This autobiography of one of America's greatest men should be known by everyone.

DU BOIS, W. E. B., *Black Reconstruction* (N. Y., 1935). The first quarter of this very interesting book contains material of value on the behavior of the slaves during the war.

DYER, BRAINERD, "The Treatment of Colored Union Troops by the Confederates, 1861-1865," *Journal of Negro History*, XX, pp. 273-286. A good piece of work. Its restraint gives it added strength.

HAY, THOMAS R., "The South and the Arming of the Slaves," *Mississippi Valley Historical Review*, VI, pp. 34-73. A good treatment of the topic.

HESSELTINE, W. B., "The Underground Railroad from Confederate Prisons to East Tennessee," *The East Tennessee Historical Society Publications*, II, pp. 55-69. An excellent paper giving much information on the aid rendered escaped Yankee prisoners by the slaves.

HIGGINSON, THOMAS W., *Army Life in a Black Regiment* (Boston, 1870). An extremely well written account by the commander of a Negro regiment in the war.

JONES, J. B., *A Rebel War Clerk's Diary*, edited by H. Swiggett, two volumes (N. Y., 1935). A day to day diary containing some material of value, particularly on the burning of Jefferson Davis' home.

LONN, ELLA, *Desertion During the Civil War* (N .Y., 1928). Contains a few incidental, but valuable, references to unity between runaway Negro bands and white guerrillas.

MARX, KARL and ENGELS, FREDERICK, *The Civil War in the United States*, (N. Y., 1937). Contains important observations on the role of the Negro.

MOORE, ALBERT B., *Conscription and Conflict in the Confederacy* (N. Y., 1934). Should be instructive to those who think the home front was unprotected during the war. Do not neglect the footnotes.

NELSON, EARL J., "Missouri Slavery, 1861-1865," in *Missouri Historical Review*, XXVIII, pp. 260-274. A good paper demonstrating the effect of the mass flight of the slaves.

OFFICIAL RECORDS *of the Union and Confederate Armies* (Washington, 1880-1901). This massive collection of 128 huge volumes is of the utmost value. It will repay careful study.

OWSLEY, FRANK L., "Local Defense and the Overthrow of the Confederacy," *Mississippi Valley Historical Review*, XI, pp. 490-525. An illuminating study for all those who still believe the South was left unprotected during the Civil War.

RANCK, JAMES B., *Albert Gallatin Brown* (N. Y., 1937). This work has a good chapter on the decision of the Confederacy to arm the Negroes.

SHANNON, FRED A., "The Federal Government and the Negro Soldier, 1861-1865," *Journal of Negro History*, IX, pp. 563-583. The treatment of the Negro soldier by the Union forces is here carefully traced.

STEPHENSON, W. H., "A Quarter-Century of a Mississippi Plantation," *Mississippi Valley Historical Review*, XXIII, pp. 355-374. Further data on the disruptive effects of the flight of the slaves.

TATUM, GEORGIA L., *Disloyalty in the Confederacy* (Chapel Hill, 1934). This is concerned with Southern white opposition to the Confederacy, but it contains a few parenthetical references to slave activity of considerable value.

WESLEY, CHARLES, "The Employment of Negroes as Soldiers in the Confederate Army," *Journal of Negro History*, IV, pp. 239-253. Contains some valuable material, but disappointing on the whole. Rather surprisingly, this Negro professor accepts the false idea that the slaves were "loyal" to the slavocracy. The same serious error mars his recent work. *The Collapse of the Confederacy* (Washington, 1937).

WILEY, BELL I., *Southern Negroes 1861-1865* (New Haven, 1938). Much pertinent material is missing, and much of that which is given is presented in an unfortunate manner. The chapters on the Negro as an individual within the Federal lines, in civil and military life, are particularly poor. Nevertheless it is the only book of its kind (an instructive commentary on the state of American historiography) and does contain a wealth of invaluable facts.

WILLIAMS, GEORGE W., *A History of the Negro Troops in the War of the Rebellion* (N. Y., 1888). A good account by a Negro participant and scholar, yet even he believed the slaves, themselves, were "docile."

WILSON, JOSEPH T., *The Black Phalanx* (Springfield, 1888). Another good military account by a Negro participant, but again the reader is told of the "docility" of the slave.

216